SOCIAL SEX

By Jason Kinkade

Contents

Introduction.. 3

Fifth Lover – Eve (Religious Coworker) 8

The Seductress (My First Adventure)..............................19

First Lover – A Hooker...27

The Grocery Store Goddess (My First Kiss) 32

Second Lover – Bailey (Stripper)..................................38

Third Lover – Chloe (Art Major)...................................44

La Bailarína (Mexico)...50

Fourth Lover – Delcine (Guatemalan Princess) 57

Susie and Shanny (The Therapeutic Group Home for Teenage Girls)..65

Sixth Lover – Faith (Married Coworker) 72

Seventh Lover – Guinevere (English Professor)...............77

Eighth Lover – Harmony (Art Teacher) 85

Ninth Lover – Isabella (Middle East Professor)................92

Tenth Lover – Jordan (Credit Union Teller) 102

Eleventh Lover – Kyra (Businesswoman) 110

Twelfth Lover – Liberty (Home Aide) 115

Thirteenth Lover – Mallory (Tango Instructor).............122

Fifteenth Lover – Ophelia (Cultural Studies Professor)..128

Fourteenth Lover – Nevaeh (Store Manager) 133

CHAPTER ONE

Introduction

Welcome to my dating book. Don't worry, there's tons of sex in it.

I am not a player. I am not macho or a stud. As far as guys go, I'm quite unexceptional in most ways. I wanted to write this book because, unlike many authors of the genre, I don't consider myself a Lothario or even very good with women. I gravitate more toward the Forever Alone types when I come to the Internet looking for an online community. I do social work for a living with an unqualified degree and am always in the lowest paying bracket of the lowest paying position. I'm 5'8" and 130 lbs. with poor vision. I'm not aggressive and don't possess a lot of qualities that immediately capture a woman's attention. Yet somehow I've made relationships with many of the most intelligent, beautiful and unique women out there. Many of them even touched my penis. And if I can do it, any man can.

It's true that without the Internet the number of women I've been with significantly drops. I received steady attention from girls throughout elementary school but didn't know what to do with it. I was flattered to be passed notes but never answered them. Anything having to do with me and the opposite sex brought my mom to make those cooing jokes about being a little heartbreaker or other comments that felt like she was mocking me and so I decided to not pursue relationships growing up. The two girls I would have broken my rule for both began dating the freakish fifth grader who went through puberty too soon. The girls that asked me out in middle school all got polite thank yous and well wishes for the future. The first girl in high school who teasingly asked me to turn around while she changed got one better and I left the room for her. All this arrested development led up to me losing my virginity to a prostitute and only having coworkers to date.

The Internet and online dating definitely deepened my dating pool but I'm still fishing for an enduring relationship. The longest lasting companionship I've ever plucked from the web is with a young New Mexican woman living nine and a half hours away from me. We've never met but we've been friends for years. Since I've known her, she's gone from being a Chili's waitress to graduating from community college with a degree in construction management. She called me when her grandmother passed away, and I leaned on her for a sympathetic ear when I quit my soul crushing job. Sometimes she is in a relationship, fewer times I am in a relationship, but we always reconnect and resume our special friendship. When she's single on Thanksgiving, she'll send me a picture or two of her ass, and, if I'm single on Christmas or New Year's, I'll get around to answering with a picture of my dick. We get each other and I hope we stay active forever. Meeting her would probably dilute this rewarding relationship.

Although I haven't found that in person meaningful relationship, the catches I've thrown back make for nearly unbelievable stories to tell.

Online love is a battlefield. I was once groomed for a traditional Mormon marriage by a woman who drove over two hours on a work night to meet me. She had never mentioned anything religious in her emails but in person quickly let me know the Bishop's role in our upcoming nuptials and her plans for the bed on wedding night. I probably would have humored her for awhile if her fingers and toes weren't still dirty from cleaning up pig shit on a farm. Then I scheduled a date for the Agave Festival at Hotel Congress with a witty sounding bartender chick. I became nervous when the day of our date arrived and she picture mailed me a steady stream of pre game photos. Why would she need to get drunk before a Tequila festival? Maybe it had something to do with her revoked license and domestic abuse charges. She had long black hair and cartoonish large breasts, and kissed me to get me to stay longer, but she also did so much drinking, shouting and crying that my escape plan involved pointing at something and running away while her head was turned.

Barack Obama's reelection night made for an enjoyable first date. The woman and I scheduled not because we were overly invested in politics but more for the event of it all. We evolved our date into us both adding on friends and brought two groups of fun people together. She and I never saw each other again but for that evening we got close, she frequently sat on my lap, and we celebrated four more years of hope and change or whatever. Another woman and I shared a really great night of bowling that started with us having to buy her a cute pair of socks from the dollar store. Except she ruined the post date momentum by sending me several pictures of her cats with names and captions as if they were having a conversation with me. As my wise coworker so eloquently summed it up: Not the kind of pussy pictures one hopes for in the middle of the night.

The women I meet from my online dating aren't just beautiful but also smart. I was once asked out by an actual medical doctor but unfortunately when we had coffee all I could think to ask her was about the accuracy of my favorite episode of House. Another woman, who I met three times and made out with on my couch after consuming her bottle of wine, had a job creating new plastics so cancer drugs wouldn't degrade between the delivery system and the human body. I suspect to be that smart in science and chemistry one also has to be deficient in other areas because that woman's social skills lagged far behind even my own. But there's been a slew of poets, teachers, librarians, and businesswomen for me to date and I've liked most of them. I don't think anybody should be persuaded away from online dating for lack of responses. Delete most the profile to increase mystery and try again. I always get the most unsolicited mail during the times I have the least to say. Most women have a million deal breakers so I don't give away my deal before I meet them. One woman arranged a date and requested we both wear dinosaur shirts. This was fun but then we talked and she told me she didn't like me. Which was awkward. But if I had written all my shortcomings online then she never would have met me, and she was smart and wrote software for a living. You never know.

This book is my complete sexual history, 15 women that slept with me and a few that didn't.

CHAPTER TWO

Fifth Lover – Eve (Religious Coworker)

The fiercest demon to escape from hell came to Earth to inhabit the body and torture the mind of the first woman for which I had overwhelming feelings. Bipolar Disorder is ugly. Its sufferers are victimized by profound mood swings that exhaust their soul and, in enough time, alienate them from even their most dedicated supporters. I'm not a doctor so to better understand my fifth lover's disease I swallowed a handful of her medication and spent hours tripping balls. When I came to, I knew she wasn't ruining our lives on purpose. Demonic possession is real.

For the first time as a college graduate, I had a job that came with a little dignity. I could come and go as I pleased, set my own schedule, and make independent decisions about how to tackle my responsibilities. I was working in a mental and behavioral health company as a case manager for children with disabilities. The system is screwed up and an entire book could be written about its problems but, for now, this summary works:

Truly evil men have figured out how to turn people's suffering into dollar signs. Workers at the very bottom, who just want to help the less fortunate, tend to trade jobs between agencies thinking the next will be better. Unfortunately, the experience is always the same. An honest worker gets assigned an enormous amount of work that nobody could possibly finish. He or she has at least two puppet middle managers that exist to demand more and more fraudulent billing. Those managers are squashed by the directors above them, telling them that their teams aren't profitable enough. The misery pours down like vomit. This description isn't coming from a disgruntled and lazy staff who got fired. I was one of the few who knew how to game the system in a way that benefited clients and made me look good. My way wasn't easy but since I was lauded as a model employee, I believe it gives me the right to make these criticisms and not be dismissed. When the time came, I quit on principle like Jerry Maguire did. I also went around and drew penises midway down everyone's yellow sticky pads, planning that I would be gone a few weeks before they started finding cocks.

When I first got hired, I was coming and going as I coordinated with schools, parents and supports for my little clients. The children on my caseload helped me more than I ever helped them. I toiled to improve their lives and they showed me great gratitude. A boy's family was so poor he only got two Hot Wheels for Christmas and of those he tried to give me one. This redeeming work that I did made me feel better about my past bad behavior.

Eve got hired after me. Eve was six years older and that only made her hotter. She was stunningly beautiful with long, curly black hair and the best body in the office. She also knew she had power over men and she loved it. I watched her get to know her team, and guys would humiliate themselves trying to welcome her or earn the right to show her how to do something. A guy a little older than her thought he was gaining interest because his jokes landed a laugh but then at the moment when it would crush him the most she announced he was so funny she was reminded of her dad. Ouch! I felt the sting from across the room.

I only got to talk to Eve when she needed a special computer terminal that was close enough to my cubicle that I became the easiest coworker to chat with during load times. During one of these occasions logging on, Eve started weeping and I genuinely asked her what was wrong. She shared quite a bit and said that she was Christian and had saved herself for marriage. Her only criteria was that her husband had to be a pastor. She settled on a music pastor (close enough) but he turned out to be fat and had a small penis. She now considered herself past her prime and without having ever been satisfied like she deserved. She just wanted to be desired and made to feel like a woman.

Some events change the course of history. A meteor wiped out the dinosaurs and allowed the ascension of mammals. The serendipitous discovery of penicillin made serious infection treatable. I told Eve that if she wanted to get laid that badly then I could be very discreet.

I regretted the words that left my mouth, thinking I was probably headed to HR for at best a sexual harassment video or at worst a pink slip, but Eve wiped away her tears and thanked me for the offer. She explained that although she saved herself for her husband and is now getting divorced she has to stay true to her Christian values and begin saving herself for her second husband. I told her that plan sounded reasonable and that I hoped she understood I was surprised by the earnestness of her story and couldn't think of a more appropriate response on the spot. At least she seemed happier, and we went about our day.

Three hours later she called me and asked me to fuck her after work.

I went to Eve's apartment in a state of shock because something like this just doesn't happen to me. Sure enough, when she opened the door and I saw lit candles all over the place I knew she hadn't changed her mind. She sat me down on the couch and clarified that she only wanted to accept half of my offer. She just wanted to make out, cuddle and be touched. She paused and added that she also wanted to be carried to the bedroom. This was turning into a whole production but I thought she was sweet and I wanted her evening to feel special so I picked her up, carried her into her room and laid her on the bed. I kissed her softly, touched her gently, and undressed her as she fell deeper and deeper into an ecstasy she claimed she had never before experienced. Turning her on was turning me on! I couldn't believe how into this she was and how she was completely losing herself to feelings she had apparently never had before. Wondering where was her real boundary, I started giving her some deeply pleasing oral sex.

The chemistry between me and Eve was amazing and probably never duplicated with anyone else. Eve was fully satisfied after our first session and I got more from going down on her than I would have from anything else. Having been mindful of her religious goal, I hadn't removed my pants or tried to penetrate her. She seemed to be playing by some rules that made sense only to her, and she bashfully told me that during our time together just now she had peeked at my erection and knew it would have felt wonderful. I told her that this intimacy could end today where we were leaving it or she could come to me again as long as she stayed comfortable with her decisions. Eve told me that we would never do this again.

I fucked Eve's pussy, ass and mouth a combined 100 times. She would ask me to pick her up before work and we'd fuck. She would ask me to meet at my apartment between appointments and we'd fuck. We would plan dates but then stay home and fuck. Eve and I could not stop fucking each other. We would take turns being deliriously horny and wake each other up in the middle of the night to fuck. Eve and I fucked. Eve wanted to fuck and be fucked in every conceivable way like she was making up for lost fucking time.

The fucking was so good that I destroyed my job, relationships, and probably impacted my sanity so much that I may never be fully sane. The first time Eve lost her mind was about a day after we put my penis in her vagina, despite her saying she wanted it and me trying to talk her out of it. We had sex at her apartment but then she came over to mine unannounced and incensed, and demanded that we get down on our knees, cry and pray to God for forgiveness. When she felt a little better she decided that we should have sex again, too.

Thus began a vicious cycle where Eve would seek me out for sex, enter a religious crisis, reach some resolution, get horny again and start over. The resolution stage usually involved me participating in a church activity with her. Clearly a charade, we would intermittently act like a couple so she could at least pretend we were committed to a godly relationship and may even get married some day. The religious crisis stage once involved Eve having her mom call me to read from the Bible. Eve's mom also gifted me an abstinence book meant for teenagers. I argued with Eve's mom that the religious upbringing was doing to the Bipolar Disorder what grease does to a fire. I firmly believe that Eve could have managed her mental health challenges more effectively without being at war with Satan and wanting to punish herself for every sin great and small. I also broke down in the same phone call with Eve's mom and professed my unyielding love for Eve. I was nuts, too.

Eve and I were two fucked up mental health workers with our own abundant mental health problems. And I regret the many times our sideshow got in the way of my ability to render service to the children and their families I was assigned to help. I knew I couldn't do my job and I assumed Eve wasn't doing hers because she spent the whole day texting me. If I put my phone away for an hour long meeting I would have 60 texts from her ranging from how much she loved me and wanted to spend her life with me to how much she despised me and which coworkers she had managed to turn against me. Work fell more askew as more coworkers witnessed and became annoyed and bothered by the lovers' quarrel between me and Eve. When events came to a head, the person who went to HR first had the upper hand.

Eve went to my boss and HR with a list of grievances. She was mad at herself but the anger and disappointment manifested in her hatred for me. She complained that I burdened and distracted her at work, and then gave a presentation on why I should be fired. Since she and I had been close, she knew that I sometimes let children from my caseload swim at my apartment pool, or that I had bought them food, paid their way into enriching events, or had done any number of things that the company training manual listed as unethical and not professional. A date was set for HR and my boss to meet with me, and I knew I was screwed. While planning my defense, I converted some angry voice mail Eve left me on my cellphone to computer audio, so threatening messages from her could play one after another on a CD. I also had a service plan and review of progress that case managers use for clients, that Eve had instead used to create behavior goals for me to direct my treatment of her in our relationship. The documentation of Eve's bipolar antics piled high.

When I sat down for my meeting, I noticed that the two women from HR had three notebooks full of rantings from Eve. I thought for a moment, strumming my fingers on my mountain of evidence, and slid it aside. I discarded everything in favor of a new and better strategic defense. I preempted HR and apologized for everything. I said I took responsibility for whatever Eve had told them, that it was all true, that Eve was an excellent staff, and that her only lapse in judgment was dating me. I told HR and my boss that I accepted my fate and to please not punish Eve. The meeting had been scheduled for 90 minutes but was over in ten.

I won the breakup.

I was not punished for anything. Eve didn't realize that management already knew I breached boundaries with clients. I made the company tons of money and could do whatever I wanted. If my car needed an oil change, I took clients with me and billed for independent skill building. If I wanted to see a movie, I took a client with me and billed for modeling appropriate behaviors in the community. The whole company was a sham operation! I wanted to spend the least amount of time on site possible and spend my days chilling in the community with cool kids who appreciated my time and thoughtful advice. My counseling in the community approach even grew into official programs that made the company that much more money. The company eventually went too far and these group outings were no longer fun for kids but that is beside the point. While trying to get me fired, Eve made herself look like a dingbat. HR declared Eve could only use the company's East office and I could only use the company's Northwest office. I hated the East office and now had a legitimate reason to miss meetings there. I preferred working in the community but in the times I absolutely had to be at the Northwest office I now knew there was no chance of running into Eve. So nice! Eve screwed herself. She struggled to build rapports with clients and families and spent nearly all her time hiding in an office. Now she wasn't allowed to be in the building closest to her apartment. Fuck you, Eve, that's what you get!

Then Eve won the breakup.

Having been Eve's second lover, and the only one she enjoyed, I never saw this coming. Eve moved on quickly and started a relationship with her high school sweetheart. She broadcast to the world that she was reunited with her soulmate. Seeing the love of your life with somebody else is an unimaginable pain. I sometimes had to drive home in the middle of my day just to sit in my apartment and be sad. I was able to function at work while in a tumultuous relationship with her but not while she was in a healthy relationship with somebody else. I had never been so depressed. And then never so angry. Eve's main criticism of me was that I wasn't Christian. She had dumped me excessively but then always came back for more sex just to break up with me again over my lack of faith. Eve had already proven herself a hypocrite many times but imagine my surprise when I learned her new boyfriend was openly living as a douchebag.

Plenty of guys believe their ex girlfriend's new man is lesser than them but that isn't the case now. For all practical purposes, the guy has me beat. He is confident, social and successful. His downfall is that he is a social media moron. I looked the guy up and he was the manager of a popular global gym. He had recently converted his Twitter account into an advertising tool for his position, forgetting that he had previously posted a plethora of date rape jokes, disparaging comments about women, racist and homophobic rants against servers and wait staff, and more pictures of beer than anyone would want to look at. That's all fine if it makes him happy but I couldn't shake all the times Eve told me I was a horrible person for not being Christian. Was this guy Christian and that made all his horrible comments OK? I printed his Twitter feed which included his recently posted coupons to new customers and previously posted gay bashing and mailed the package to his corporate boss. Fired. I guess, Christian or not, that shit is not OK. Of all the men Eve could have replaced me with, she chose a meat head body builder that publishes hate speech online.

Eve and I were never face to face again after HR separated us, and it took three years before I could go a full day without thinking about her. I believe she took on the personality of her new boyfriend and his exercise cult because I saw a couple pictures of her down the road, and her once beautiful body was now overly muscular and gross. If Eve needed CrossFit as a new obsession to replace reading the Bible then everything worked out for the best. I know she will always have Bipolar Disorder but without her soul hanging in the balance of every decision she can probably live her life and be happy.

I try not to think about her but I vividly remember a time I thought she was going to scream at me but she instead sat me down and gave me deeply pleasing oral sex. We knew each other's bodies but not each other's minds.

CHAPTER THREE

The Seductress (My First Adventure)

The Internet ruined my life. When it was new, however, I thought it was something akin to Prometheus stealing fire from the gods. My life online felt better. I was able to construct an entire social life in cyberspace. I hung out on message boards, specifically one based around a popular animated action cartoon, and developed complex friendships with the other posters. There were two teenage girls in the mix, and with my witty comments and the sheer volume of time spent logged in I was able to monopolize the attention of the most desired female user. When she started calling me on the phone, too, I knew I had to meet her and begin my own happily ever after.

I was a senior in high school when I struck up an inappropriate relationship with a girl online. Her story was that she was the daughter of a visiting Japanese professor teaching at one of the universities in California. Unlike with girls in real life, I could talk to her very easily across a range of shared interests. She sent me naked pictures which caused me to feel very possessive of her. Whereas I should have blocked her from communicating with my screen name, my mind blocked out the obvious reality that she was an attention starved brat teasing boys online. I was also 17 closer to 18 while she was still 16 closer to 15. This was all so wrong but at the time felt so right.

The Seductress, a very cute Japanese teenager, gave me her address and implored me to come have sex with her. This was incredibly dangerous behavior but at least she chose me since I'm more of an idiot than a predator. I was wrongly under the impression that she and I had a real bond and would probably start dating and enjoy adult lives together. I needed to make some things happen before I could go see her and I got right to work. First, I had to get a driver's license. I hadn't yet because I hadn't had anywhere to go. My life revolved around the computer. Second, I had to get a car. Most teens dream of owning a car but I couldn't have cared less. Third, I had to get a map and find Orange County.

I had never driven to the park or library before but I was on my way to Laguna Beach. I'm embarrassed to be aware that as an angst filled teenager I could so easily be handed the keys to a new Dodge Stratus and yet believe I was born with the cards stacked against me. I thought life had treated me unfairly and that I unduly suffered from acne, social anxiety, physical weakness and other setbacks I could have overcome with minimal effort. At any rate, I thought meeting the Seductress was fate turning my life around. I told my parents I was going to spend some days sleeping at my buddy's house, and I told my buddy that I was going to go meet my future wife.

I turned a nine hour drive into an 18 hour drive. I had no idea what I was doing on the road. Driving was hard and navigating was harder! When I got to the Holiday Inn in Orange County I took the longest hot shower of my life. I stood in the water and steamed out. I was very stressed and suddenly scared of where I was and what I was doing. When I got settled into my room, I set up my laptop and tried to coordinate with the Seductress but she was suddenly nowhere to be found online. Using the technology of the time, I was still able to rig my devices so that any contact from her would ping my bulky Nokia cellphone. I got dressed as nicely as I could and then started resting on the couch, waiting for her to cross my radar.

The Seductress never attempted to reach me. She knew I was coming and now she was mysteriously missing from all of our online hangouts. As the hotel charged me $10 for each dial up connection it slowly dawned on me that the Seductress may have been full of shit. Maybe pleading for me to come make love to her was just something she said online to guys for kicks. My buddy had warned me of this possibility and I waved him off. Except, I had her home address and wanted to know what was going on for sure. She had sent me naked pictures, told me she wished we were in the same room, and encouraged me to come get her. I came this far and wanted an answer.

My awake and sleep times were off because of the drive but I got to the Seductress's house sometime in the early evening. I called her on the phone and left her a message that I was outside her house. I told her

I was going to ring her doorbell and ask her parents to get her for me if she didn't explain herself. She called back immediately and chewed me out. She called me a pervert, a stalker, a freak, a loser, a psycho and worse. She said only a fool would fall in love with naked pictures and drive from Arizona to California to meet a minor. She kept stressing that she was a minor and I was nearly an adult which was probably how she actually felt now that somebody from her online deception had appeared in person. Again, her being lucky she picked me, I saw this disappointing turn of events as the end of the line. I was as likely to rape her as I was to sprout wings and fly to Valhalla. I figured I'd go back to my hotel, order pizza and watch TV.

Then the Seductress called me with a change of heart. She sweetly told me that she would see me if I would first go buy her some crystal meth. I said sure why not and asked how to go about buying drugs. She didn't have a really good answer but suggested I go see a Hispanic girl from her class that lived in Alhambra. The Hispanic girl seemed cool (except for being a teenage addict) and got in my car as soon as I said I was on a mission to buy meth. It seemed silly, but the Hispanic girl coached me to start telling people I was Persian and from Iran. Apparently, her connections would take issue with her bringing a white guy into the hood. Soon enough, I had three attractive Hispanic girls in my car and we were driving around their usual route to pickup expensive psycho-stimulants.

The Hispanic girls didn't know I was a dweeb from the Internet and kept telling me that I had the nicest car of anyone they knew. I told them I made good money as a drug dealer in Arizona and that I was out here looking for new drugs I could introduce back at my high school. I was feeding them so much bullshit and they kept graciously eating it. I also didn't have time for all this no left turn signage posted everywhere in Southern California which made the Hispanic girls think of me as that much more of a rebel. When we finally scored some meth, I had to wonder why I spent all my money on such a small amount of white stuff. The whole culture of these teens seemed ridiculous. We spent so long scurrying around like little rats looking for cheese when we could have been doing any number of other things. My hotel alone probably had ten better things to do.

When I said goodbye to the Hispanic girls, I was overcome with a notion of striking comedy gold and announced that I was a DEA agent and they were all under arrest. One of them cried. Oops. They left absolutely pissed, and all of my reassurances that I was just kidding did nothing to make up for my humor. I learned that these teens also have to live in fear of ruining their lives and invoking the wrath of their parents and grandparents. High School in Orange County was so laughable! I was starting to think that I should just go home and be glad I don't live like this. I took my share of the crystal meth and repackaged it in a micro VHS tape case since I felt like the little plastic baggie was going to blow away.

That's how drug dealers from Arizona go the extra mile.

This time when I called the Seductress she answered. She opened her front door for me, now late at night, and whisked me into her room. Goddamn it. She did look like a minor. And after everything I had just gone through, I felt more like an adult than ever before. She was very attractive but her excessive makeup that looked sexy in pictures now made her look like a little girl trying to appear older. She was shy but grateful for the drugs. She wasted no time getting her meth pipe and invited me to smoke with her in her bedroom. I had never done drugs before (and never have again) but I spent several hours with the Seductress smoking crystal meth and laughing about all the inside jokes that grew out of our message board interactions. I actually had fun and abandoned all intention of having sex with her.

When I finally got back to my hotel in the early morning, I was super high on crystal meth and cleaned the dirt and grime out of my room. I didn't have many spare minutes to get checked out, dispute the excessive Internet fees, and head over to the Seductress's private high school where she had asked me to meet her. She had assembled a group of her friends and introduced me, again, as the Arizona drug dealer. I was already tiring of this act and feeling like I deserved an introduction on my own merits. The Seductress's male friends were asking me very specific questions about selling drugs in school and I just kept making up answers that sounded right to me.

If they wanted to stay in touch I readily gave them my email address. The Seductress's female friends kept praising me for being smart and handsome. My confidence grew and I felt even more anxious to go home and start working on myself. I began believing I could have this attention and social success without the phony backdrop of being a drug dealer if I just learned to project confidence for real.

After I hugged the Seductress goodbye, one of her also Asian and very beautiful female friends informed me that she was having a ditch day and wanted to hang out. This was a sultry suggestion so I accepted her company and took her off campus. The friend and I had a nice afternoon together in the O.C. We went to the beach, lunch and walked around trendy shopping destinations. The friend shamelessly flirted with me, hugged on me, and at one time jumped on me for a sexy piggyback ride. The friend and I essentially shared an awesome date though I don't consider it such since the hearts floating in her eyes were because she thought I was a drug dealer and was attracted to that perception of power and prestige. The friend told me that she was interested in trying harder drugs and that she wanted me to be her teacher.

I did the math once, and as an adult with counseling credentials I have so far mentored 180 teenagers. When the friend asked me to introduce her to harder drugs, I turned into my true self and told her no. She was taken aback, but I lobbed some more lies at her to get to a more important truth. I told her that I regretted having gone down this path selling drugs and that substances really can ruin a life. I told her there is a special place in hell for drug dealers and that she should consider the people who have invested in her, or little family members that may look up to her, and work on making her dreams a reality. I told her we all have dreams and that we need to be working on them in the here and now rather than some faraway day. I said there is always something we can do today that will pull tomorrow's ultimate goal a little closer. I asked her to think about herself just a few years ago and consider whether she aspired to be ditching class with a drug dealer. The friend didn't outright resist this advice and we still shared a nice drive back to her school. I got to say goodbye to the Seductress again who had by now tired of my drug dealer schtick and resented the undeserved adoration I received from her classmates. If I got through to the friend then my trip was worth it.

To drive back to Arizona, I first pulled into a gas station and asked for directions. The foreign clerk wrote a route for me on the back of register tape and I got home without issue. I ordered a pizza and watched TV. As I began telling my buddy and his friends about my adventure, they all came up with the same question. They always wanted to know why I never smoked pot with them but so eagerly smoked crystal meth with a slutty Asian teenager. And I always had the same answer:

Gateway drugs are for pussies.

CHAPTER FOUR

First Lover – A Hooker

My first sexual encounter cost $80. I graduated from a private Christian academy and had still never kissed a girl. The religious environment wasn't to blame for my inexperience with women, I was just socially awkward. To that point, I had already bounced around five or so regular high schools.

One night, my buddy and I were house sitting for my mom's gay friends and somewhere between watching the movies Zoolander and The Time Machine we got the idea to log onto America Online and troll chat rooms for babes. We really wanted to make the most of our time in a very nice house but, despite multiple screen names and tactics, this endeavor yielded no results. At the behest of my buddy, we drove across town to an apartment belonging to a group of his friends. By now, I think he had lost interest in finding girls and just wanted to smoke marijuana.

This was an important buddy of mine because he accepted me and all my shortcomings. Thanks to his social capital and goodwill, the other guys put up with me. All these guys, like my buddy, were pretty experienced with girls and already into furthering their educations or getting jobs. You know, normal people. I, however, had no post high school plans but to exist like a bump on a log. It was pretty awkward that I never did drugs, never had money, never had female companions, and never had anything interesting to contribute to the group. Still, my buddy brought me along and set the tone that everyone should tolerate me despite my missing personality. On this particular night, my buddy rallied the group to find me a prostitute.

Calling a hooker in Tucson, Arizona is surprisingly easy. All one has to do is pick up a free newspaper, any from the array of advertisement filled rags that hire journalism students or hippies to write about local music and liberal politics, and start thumbing through the blatant sex ads. Inside one of these publications, my buddy and his friends called a few women offering personal massages and left them messages to sort out which were actually offering sex (all of them). As hoes or their pimps started returning calls, this benevolent group of guys booked a lady and came up with her fee.

Now, I really only wanted to have sex for the first time so I would no longer have to dread fielding questions about my sexual experience level from peers or people at times with whom I was forced to speak. Even in a religious high school that promoted abstinence, those kids while in classroom table groups or at other inappropriate times would aim to humiliate me by asking if I was a virgin. With this prostitute experience behind me, I hoped I could move on with my life. And my plan for living was to never venture very far from home. I considered the last godawful 12 years of academics all that should ever be asked of me.

I wasn't nervous waiting for the prostitute but I should have been. Little did I know, my first spectacular sexual failure was just minutes away. I still wasn't nervous even in the seconds after we all heard that much anticipated knock on the front door. The guys answered and sure enough there was a hooker and her much shorter and white middle aged pimp. I felt guilty for assuming he was going to be black and look cool. Money exchanged hands and the little pimp said he would be back in an hour.

The hooker asked who she was going to fuck and every finger in the now silent room pointed at me. She glanced my way and said OK. I stared at her for longer and decided that I was happy with how she looked. I knew back before anyone opened the newspaper she wasn't going to look like Julia Roberts or Elisabeth Shue but thankfully she actually looked like a normal woman from any given day. She was shapely, had nice blond hair, a cute outfit, and couldn't have been more than ten years older than me. Not bad. I can work with this, I thought. She asked my buddy to put music on, lower the lights and get the room cleared.

My hooker started undressing to Pink Floyd's Learning to Fly while I sat on the couch and watched. The most fun I had was when she sauntered over to me and put my hands over her breasts. I had never touched any before and they were amazing. I kept circling those tits with open palms, squeezing, and raising then dropping her nipples over my fingers. Next, I was a little put off when she stood tall, turned around, slipped her skirt to her ankles, and bent over to reveal that wedged in her crack was underwear bearing Winnie the Pooh. Childhood: Assassinated. The Disney panties came off soon enough and she was totally naked, kneeling before me, rubbing my crotch and unzipping my pants.

I think my trouble actually began with Internet pornography. My boner was accustomed to coming out for pixels and not real women. When I realized my hooker wasn't going to give me an erection, I got angry and started thinking about now having to answer for being a virgin and having a scared penis. This is when I also began noticing the not-so-sexy ambiance. My buddy and his friends were enjoying video games in the other room, and from the sound effects I could make out which titles and what levels they were playing. Some jackass was even trying to watch me by lying on the floor and using the reflection in a CD as a mirror.

My hooker, ever the professional, was still telling me that my flaccid dick was big and making her horny and all this nonsense I recognized as customer service. I surprised myself with attitude and assertiveness and bluntly told her she needed to shut the fuck up if I was ever going to be attracted to her. I instructed her to dance for awhile, which she did to perfection, while I rubbed myself to no avail. I just wanted to get hard and put on one of the many condoms she had brought with her and get to having sex in front of an audience of peers who could then act as witnesses. Finally, I told my hooker to get into a doggy style position, I rolled a condom over my limp dick and rubbed the junk all over her butt and pussy.

Mission accomplished. I figured I got the tip in a little bit and I could tell people I had sex and it wouldn't be a lie. I got dressed. She got dressed. We flicked the lights on and opened the room. My buddy looked at the clock and stopped my hooker from leaving. He informed her that she had been present for 45 minutes but that he had paid for an hour. I thought that was shockingly badass of him, and went into the other room as the guys filled up the room I had just been in.

I had some video games to play, and my first lover had some dicks to suck.

CHAPTER FIVE

The Grocery Store Goddess (My First Kiss)

At the ripe age of 21, I got mad at my parents and ran away from home. We were probably fighting about me not wanting to go to college. I left while they were at a Chinese restaurant and didn't tell them where I was going to live. My buddy that always helped me out, set me up at his girlfriend's house. His girlfriend had a sweet deal living with a girl friend whose parents were supposedly teaching her life lessons by paying for a large home and having her pay a small rent. I had my own room, bathroom and walk-in closet. I slept on the floor but foolishly felt like I had won the lottery.

These young women I now lived with expected me to at some point get on my feet and start contributing but put absolutely no pressure on me. My buddy also offered to cover some of my expenses. Looking back, all these people I grew up with were incredibly decent. My buddy was a selfless giver but I thought he was dumb for not knowing mathematics and grammar. I had always looked down on him and his other friends because they did drugs and, in most cases, their parents weren't as successful as mine. But all these kids grew up right and cared for each other. I probably should have gotten my hands dirty and done some drugs with them which seemed to be an important unifying experience. It would have crushed my parents but this crushed them, too.

On my first day as an adult runaway, I walked into a grocery store and asked for a job. And got one. All that was asked of me was to cut my shoulder length long hair. My buddy bought me a nice haircut at one of those barbershops where the men go all out, are excited about sports, have cigars and debate the news. I couldn't remember the last time I had short hair but I was surprised how handsome it made me look. The long hair had helped me conceal acne and disappear from the spotlight in class but when my face cleared up I never thought to show it off. When I started working, I got attention from females, too.

I began as a courtesy clerk making $5 an hour. I had never worked before but much preferred it to high school. I brought carts in and talked to the other courtesy clerks, mostly kids much younger than me or an adult with a mental health disability. One lowly functioning coworker wanted to corner people and talk about movies all day. I'd entertain him by having the same conversation over and over about how great of a film was Charlie's Angels: Full Throttle. He had a heart of gold. For the most part, I worked hard at my job and it got recognized. In just eight days I was promoted to the bakery. Promotions weren't meant to come until 90 days but suddenly I had earned an apron, $8 and talk of cake decorator school.

The female attention I got in the bakery was mostly from old women shoppers making cliched comments about how nice were my buns. They would also slip money into my apron so I flirted right back to remain profitable. We were the only 24 hour store, so strippers would come in late to buy milk with all their one dollar bills. I would go bag up their few items and offer them help out. Some of the women coworkers were attractive but a much despised new employee took my breath away. Many established employees wanted the customer service position because it was generally considered easy in this store but it ultimately went to some district manager's niece who came from the outside with no work experience. She had curly brown and blond hair, a petite build, an impressive rack, those shiny and wet lips, and a pattern of moles on both temples that kind of reminded me of a babe from Star Trek.

This Grocery Store Goddess wasn't the only unique colleague of mine. An older cashier who was always charming customers and coworkers took me to a bar one night and told me he used to be a coal miner with a modest but enjoyable life. He said starting over as a bagger in a grocery store was embarrassing but life is tough and he has no regrets. I preferred him to the produce guy who asked me if I knew any girls that would shoot pornography for him at his house. After the cashier and I had a few drinks at the bar we went back to his unfurnished apartment. All he had was a huge American flag on the wall. He smoked crack all night while I drank vodka and listened to his stories. Somehow he was picture perfect in the morning and I felt like shit.

After a few weeks, the Grocery Store Goddess was still universally disliked, unapproachable and stuck up. I don't know how my balls descended but I announced over the intercom that she needed to dial the bakery. She did right away and I asked her if she wanted to come with me and the cashier to the bar after work. To my genuine surprise, she immediately said yes and then walked back to my bakery for directions and to warn me that she was going to go home first and change.

The cashier and I got to the bar first but soon the Grocery Store Goddess came in looking sexy and actually bought me a drink. She was also 21 and like me she seemed unsure of what to do with herself. Except for drinking of which she did a lot. The cashier pointed for me to turn around and look at what she was doing and she had racked pool balls up backwards. I was a little drunk, too, so I slapped her ass and started seeing what else I could try with her. With the night grinding on, the conversation between me and the Grocery Store Goddess dulled into gibberish and she finally asked impatiently if I was going to kiss her.

Without hesitation, I kissed this Grocery Store Goddess. It didn't mean anything to her but I kissed her with feeling and my heart exploded with joy. My romantic experience to date included sex with a prostitute but I had never kissed a girl. I'll always prefer first kisses with someone special to anything else including sex. A kiss is the first barrier that comes down when two people are getting to know each other. Sex is sometimes even a chore or something both parties know has to happen before a relationship is to be made. A kiss isn't expected and doesn't have to happen at all. I kissed my Grocery Store Goddess and it remains one of my greatest achievements.

The Grocery Store Goddess's shine dimmed a little after she invited me back to her place. Her place was gross and her three giant dogs immediately jumped all over me until she poured a bag of dog food on the floor for them to attack the scattered pieces. She warned me that we weren't having sex yet but then she took her clothes off and lied in bed with me. Except now she wanted to show me yearbook pictures and tell me about her glory days as a cheerleader. Not knowing how to make moves yet, I went along with what descended into her pity party and then us having to go introduce me to her sister for some unknown reason. I left that morning not having had sex and really confused but figured it would all make sense later when we were dating.

Except she ignored me from then on out and I never got the time of day from her again. I still had a lot to learn about women and now know that just because they let you kiss them or even more it doesn't guarantee a damn thing. Women are just people and everyone goes through rough patches and sometimes some physical comfort is needed for just one drunken night. It certainly can't be easy being the reviled niece of a district manager working a perceived better job amongst the unwashed masses. Still, having gained and then lost the affection of the Grocery Store Goddess was hard on me. The weeks beat me up and my relatively stress free job was monotonous and boring. I came from wealthy parents and was now one of the working poor whose checks were spent on bills way before payday.

During a shift like any other, a quiet middle aged Indian woman who closed the deli every night that I closed the bakery grabbed me and with an angry face told me I was an idiot. She said if I had parents who were willing to pay for college then I needed to leave the grocery store right now and go back home. She looked hurt and told me that she had been in the deli many years, will be there many more, she and her son suffer, and that this is not a life. She was the real grocery store goddess.

To her: Thank you.

CHAPTER SIX

Second Lover – Bailey (Stripper)

I had only ever kissed one girl but I did have sex with a prostitute by the time I started dating a stripper. Bailey was a full blooded Apache woman who her customers knew as Queen Cobra. I didn't go to clubs but I had become aware of Bailey through friends. On at least two occasions, we were at my buddy's house at the same time but never spoke. I was living at home with my parents again after having run away and subsequently burning out working at a grocery store. I was now in a community college and, thanks to some inspiring professors, actually enjoying academics for the first time. Bailey was a sexy woman but had pain and trouble beneath her surface. She was my first pseudo girlfriend and helped me grow in a lot of ways.

Hitting on Bailey was surprisingly easy. Some friends from my expanding circle had been taking me to karaoke nights for awhile. There was a bar for college kids we would go to one night a week and on another night there was a bar for the working class. I preferred the latter, with its decent rock and roll or sad love songs versus the poppy stuff wailed over and over by sorority girls. One night in the blue collar bar, I saw Bailey drinking alone. Her purse was clear plastic and filled with crumpled dollars. Her high heels were clipped between the rungs of her bar stool and she appeared to be concealing a stripper outfit with only a coat. Since she probably had seen me at least once before in neutral territory I felt it was reasonable to approach her.

I tripped and hit my face on her shoulder when I tried to sit by her. Luckily, she thought it was cute and did recognize me. We struck up a conversation about the friends we kept in common and then I awkwardly asked what she did for a living. She didn't seem offended but asserted that I already knew she was a stripper. She then goaded me on to ask questions she assumed I must have had. I told her I didn't have a question other than if I could take her out sometime. She accepted and wrote her number on a napkin for me. I thought this was all smooth and well played, like a scene from a movie, even though it must happen in bars all over the country all of the time. I told my friends that I was going to take Bailey on a date and they stifled some laughter and warned me that she might be a little crazy.

She didn't seem that crazy at first. Bailey told me that she liked exotic dancing because she likes to sleep in and appreciates flexible hours. She also had bad experiences from more traditional entry level jobs, such as the time she claimed a robber came into Little Caesar's and tied her to a toilet while he emptied the register. She said she feels more safe in the strip club because the bouncers protect her. I never had any interest in seeing her perform on a stage so I never went inside her work but I did on occasion pick her up. I'd foolishly ask the bouncers to go fetch her for me and they would sternly tell me to fuck off. I realized that I couldn't retrieve my stripper date from her place of business because the outside staff assumed I was a stalker from the street. She would come out eventually, always smiling and happy to see me.

Our first couple dates were mundane, with me taking her to restaurants then dropping her off at home. I was mimicking dating scenarios I saw on bland TV shows and still didn't know how to escalate things when dating a woman. Bailey was the first woman I had ever taken on a date and I was hoping that she would give me a clear indication that she wanted to take things further. If I had known what constituted a woman's interest, I may have considered it a good sign that her dresses were so short we had to strategically accept or reject certain seating by whether or not other patrons could see her vagina. What I did notice, was that when a man walks into a restaurant with a stripper on his arm the male wait staff pays him a lot of respect. Never before or again have I been referred to so politely and so frequently by my surname.

For some reason, I thought acting gentlemanly would cause Bailey to ask me to have sex with her. Like, if I showed disinterest a little longer she may very well demand I look at her naked. It was probably while dropping her off after the second date that I tried to give her more time to make a decision by asking to use her bathroom. Fearing that she may be less enthused to suck my dick if she heard a urine stream,

I qualified my request by saying I only needed to wash my hands. Then I closed the door and peed in her sink. She didn't make a move on me and I again left with nothing.

While attempting to drop Bailey off after a third date, she started feigning panic that she might not have a key. I somehow knew that when she asked me to wait while she checked if her roommate was home that she was going to come back and claim she couldn't get inside. The scenario quickly played out as I imagined and she asked if she could sleep over. I figured that my parents would be asleep, that I could manage the dogs, and that somehow all of this would work out and I would finally get laid. I was hoping for real sex. I had only ever fruitlessly struggled to penetrate a hooker's vagina with my flaccid penis. Now I had a scorching hot Native American going on real dates with me. Progress.

We got inside my room stealthily and sat on my bed to talk. I attempted to make out with her but had only ever kissed one girl from my grocery store. Fortunately, Bailey seemed down to teach and asked that I slow the pace of my kisses and open my mouth a little so she could introduce her tongue. I enjoyed this and felt a natural erection rise in my pants. I started thinking about the condoms I had in my dresser and how all of this was supposed to unfold. I figured I would try and have sex with her straight away because I wanted to know what she really felt like and only go for the condoms if she requested them. Except, I still didn't know how to run to the next base even with a willing woman lying in my bed teaching me how to make out. The kisses dried up and she asked me to go get her a soda.

As I sneaked back with a carbonated beverage, I realized I was losing momentum and probably about to hear that she wanted to go home. Then she informed me she was going to drink her Coke and watch me masturbate. That was an unexpected turn of events but I eagerly complied and stroked slowly so she could finish her drink. When she set it aside, I calculated the phrase with the highest probability of success, flip flopped on going in without a condom, and remarked that I had protection nearby and needed her help to finish. She said good idea. Game time!

Bailey took her clothes off which required a lot of unzipping and we got to having sex. If there was ever a question about losing my virginity to a prostitute then there was certainly none that I lost it to a stripper. I penetrated her in the missionary position and then doggy style. I didn't know what I was doing and just thrust away, changing positions as she requested. The experience was not necessarily enjoyable and I couldn't feel anything but my simultaneous pride and disappointment. I had never put a condom on my erection before for longer than a quick and curious test while alone and couldn't finish. I could tell despite some low moans that Bailey probably wasn't having a blast either. We peeled off the condom and finished me with a hand job. I didn't do anything for her and seriously didn't know that something was probably expected.

First thing in the morning, Bailey wanted to take a dump, use my computer to look at death and autopsy photos, and cry a river about how I am not attracted to her and probably won't marry her. I tried to take her to breakfast but apparently the hostess gave her attitude and needed to be shouted at until we were asked to leave. Finally, we had to fill Dr. Pepper bottles with rum so she could drink heavily at work. She also casually mentioned her boyfriend was coming back to town. She had been bat shit crazy all along, I just couldn't see it until after I fucked her.

CHAPTER SEVEN

Third Lover – Chloe (Art Major)

Sweet little Chloe. I was such an introvert in high school and then unexpectedly started doing all kinds of exciting things at Pima Community College. I was making at least one amazing friend in every class and had plenty of downtime in my schedule to spend with these new people. I was growing socially until, as contradictory as it may sound, getting my first real girlfriend amounted to taking an enormous step backward.

Early on, I cobbled together an original animated short and with the help of friends I only knew through the Internet got it hosted online. My movie wasn't well written, drawn or acted but crude cartoons with needless profanity hadn't yet permeated every corner of the world wide web, and I suddenly had a modicum of success on my hands. Thanks to my website, I also had a forum with a following, was offered a small weekly column in the statewide newspaper, attended two animation conventions to be received by real fans, and got invited to a local film festival and after party.

I met Chloe at the party. She was the freshly dumped former girlfriend of the host. He was a charming and handsome freshman and he and Chloe had been high school sweethearts in Gilbert, Arizona. Their small town relationship ended abruptly when they both moved to the University of Arizona and he realized he wanted to bang hotter women. Chloe was allowed to stay his friend and stuck around because she couldn't think of anything better to do than torture herself. Chloe was not adapting to higher education and missed the simpler days she left behind in hay country. I was introduced to her at the party and spent a lot of time with her because of the attention given to me by the host and her orbiting him at all times.

Chloe was pretty plain looking and often described her own style as frumpy. My buddy pushed me into asking for her number, with which she obliged and stamped into my phone, but I was never that enthusiastic about her. I kissed her that night more because I knew I could than because of any other reason. I was a celebrity from the attention my creative endeavor attracted and felt entitled to some party favor. I shouldn't have called Chloe but I asked her on a date. On my way to pick her up I couldn't remember if she was attractive to me or not and hoped that in a more brightly lit environment she would be cute. She wasn't. She had prepared for the date by applying makeup, a skill she hadn't honed or practiced.

If Chloe were the math problem one plus one solve for a boyfriend then any answer was correct. It took all of half a dinner date for Chloe to transfer her full affection from her high school sweetheart onto me. There was no pulling a conversation out of her and I was fighting with time until I could return her to her dorm. She raised her courage in my car when she recognized the turns I was making and voiced that she wasn't ready to go home, which put me back at a loss for what to even do with her. I drove Chloe to my buddy's house and had beers with him while she sat there and awkwardly remained silent but happy. She told me she had a magnificent time.

After Chloe overextended our date, I finally managed to get her back to her dorm and she invited me inside. Walking up those stairs, I knew Chloe would chomp at the bit to be my girlfriend and I considered that for the first time in my life I would have a reliable wellspring of sex. Even with this prospect, I knew a better way to go would be to hold out for a girl for whom I was more attracted. We got to Chloe's dorm and I met her two goofy roommates. The room looked uncomfortably small and without any personal privacy. My tour included the hallway restroom which was disgusting and where I learned that students living in the dorms see each other shit and wear flip flops to take a shower. None of this was anything of which I wanted to take part.

Now that Chloe was comfortable with me, she called and asked me to see her again. I returned to her dorm during the day with every intention of dumping her. I didn't have any experience severing a budding relationship and we took a walk that lasted so long it eventually felt like the wrong time to cut her loose. I resolved to dump Chloe later by email. Chloe kind of teased that we may be alone when we got back to her dorm and then of course we weren't. She let me know that she was sorry and would make it up to me. Before I could dump her, she told me that she was going home for the summer and for a week while her parents were still vacationing would have the house to herself.

Chloe's parents' house where she lived that summer was two hours away from me and she couldn't drive nor had access to a car. I therefore figured that I could have sex with her that first week and then the relationship would naturally expire because of logistical challenges that weren't anyone's fault. I could even sign up for summer school to suffocate and squeeze the life out of our long distance relationship. So I fucked Chloe and to my surprise she was amazing! When I can relax, go without pressure, and take the time needed to experience a woman's body the sex is pure bliss. Chloe, my third lover, set a high bar for future sexual partners. I wasn't attracted to her face, personality or style but come to find out there were parts under the clothes of which I couldn't get enough. Chloe and I probably didn't leave the bed that week. Her vagina was pink and beautiful.

Feeling fully satisfied, I was ready for my first girlfriend, Chloe, to disappear into the annals of history. Then I learned that her father was an amateur pilot and she was able to come visit me all summer via dad's hobby aircraft. Absolutely dumbfounded by this development, I went to pick up Chloe from a rink-a-dink airport by me which I had never previously known about but was now at having breakfasts and lunches with her family. Who the hell is free to fly their daughter from Gilbert to Tucson and back all summer so she can see her boyfriend? Apparently her dad owned this plane with two other dorks and the three of them shared access to it. Spending time with Chloe started depressing me more than when I didn't even have a girlfriend. For instance, she found it cute when she'd notice something like having put her big panties on inside out but I would just be more and more turned off by her frumpy awkwardness.

Chloe was an art student but not an artist. She wouldn't share any of her work with me and expressed being embarrassed by her lack of talent. She didn't know why she was in college and didn't aspire to anything. I was meeting interesting women in class all the time and, perhaps wrongfully, assumed that without Chloe as my ball and chain could probably get to know a young woman that could capture my heart and mind. Or at least wouldn't at all times make me feel like shoving my head through a small airplane's spinning propeller blades. Chloe came back after the summer and rented an apartment near the University of Arizona. She complained of being lonely and used the carrot of sex to keep me staying over until I devised my best plan to date.

As a solution to Chloe's loneliness that didn't involve me, I bought her a pet hamster with all the needed accessories and dumped her. She flunked out of college and moved back home. I had been cruel to her for the duration of our relationship but soon enough the universe rewarded her with a doting husband that thought she was in fact interesting. He was a professional helicopter pilot and they wasted no time buying a house and making babies. Chloe had flashed into my life during a deceptive burst of success that subsided just as quickly, and I would go through a two year dry spell before I got close to a woman again. I only watched for a little while, but Chloe's rising star took her higher than anywhere I was going. I lived at home, was already older than most my classmates, and woefully uninformed about community college graduation requirements as I learned when I tried to apply for a degree with nothing but elective credits and was laughed out of the office. Sweet little me.

CHAPTER EIGHT

La Bailarína (Mexico)

I did a lot of stupid things when I thought I was famous. I maintained a popular website and moderated its forum while in community college, and with two feet jumped on any opportunity that reinforced my belief that I was some kind of Internet celebrity. I went to a party that celebrated my animated movies and left that night with a needy girlfriend that followed me around in an airplane, and, almost as ridiculously, I allowed a self important neck bearded teenager to come from Nebraska with his hopes of receiving my training and success in life. I'm not sure if that makes me or him the bigger dumbass.

Neckbeard wrote to me from (guessing) a cornfield and introduced himself as a fast fan of my animation who was also warming up to my political humor blog. Since I wrote about Arizona, he suggested he start a related blog for his Midwestern state and that in time we could attract other like-minded webmasters from around the country. I told him to go ahead but then had to laugh at the inferior quality of everything he uploaded. Not that my content was that great but I was affiliated with a newspaper and had a professional looking layout combined with a mindfulness about current events and unique perspective. Everything Neckbeard did looked sloppy and full of failure, and I had to renege on my agreement to link to each other. Of note, however, is that my only and younger brother was never a fan of my work and ranked Neckbeard's site superior because of its unintended humor and bold illiteracy.

I was a community college student living at home with my parents, and Neckbeard was a high school graduate working in a factory while living at home with his parents. Although Neckbeard was turning 20 he looked much older, like a 40 year old man knocked around by life. He was obese, freckled and with red hair and a patchy beard. When he said he wanted to come to Arizona, like it would be an Internet worthy event, I jokingly said OK but then watched in shock as he booked a flight and made plans to stay at my house. My parents were surprisingly supportive when I broke the strange news that a fat man from Lincoln was going to stay in our guestroom, or they may have been encouraged and fooled by this supposed professional networking conference after my underwhelming adolescence. My brother was stoked because he rightfully guessed Neckbeard was going to be as awkward and cringe worthy in person as he was online.

I knew I was in trouble when Neckbeard lumbered off the plane and revealed he doesn't make it very far before crashing into something. He is just totally oblivious to his size and surroundings and able to spill, drop, break and ruin anything and everything of which he comes into contact. Although my brother was out on his own long before me, he turned up at the restaurant for Neckbeard's inaugural dinner with the family, and to this day laughs when he recalls how sad Neckbeard looks when the food is gone. My brother finding Neckbeard amusing was a fortunate break for me because I was able to hide in my summer school Astronomy class, saying we had planet gazing assignments that were going to take all day and night. I just couldn't take large doses of Neckbeard. My brother and his friends took Neckbeard golfing one afternoon, which necessitated a hunt for an XXL collared polo that resolved when the back of my dad's closet produced an improperly sized logo shirt sent to him by mistake. The family once laughed that this red shirt was large enough to raise on a flagpole. The funniest thing to do with Neckbeard is take him somewhere outside and wait for his whiny rants on how inhumane it is to bake a fat man in the sun.

Neckbeard made himself comfortable at my computer and spent so much time at my desk that I hardly logged on anywhere while he was staying with me. Then by chance I checked the message board from school and was upset to find Neckbeard broadcasting about me and making me look bad. He wasn't doing so maliciously but he started too many threads about his every idiotic observation, so mixed in with his announcements that he saw his first saguaro cactus and tried Arizona Iced Tea were comments on how I was shorter than he expected and my girlfriend wasn't pretty. People were already laughing out loud and speculating that Neckbeard and I were gay lovers. I shouldn't have cared what people from the Internet thought but at the time worried Neckbeard was going to ruin my reputation and drive members away from my forum. When Neckbeard made a creepy request, I worriedly decided I needed to help him out lest he make more disappointing disclosures. Basically, Neckbeard confessed never having done anything with a woman and asked if I could help him make inroads with the fairer sex before he returned to Nebraska. I reasoned that if I could get this fat bastard laid then he would report it online, win back the defectors, and then the overall astonished masses would think I possessed super powers.

I saw a single shortcut to success and drove Neckbeard into Mexico. I didn't know how this was supposed to work exactly but heard rumors that the sex was going to flow to us. Soon enough, a shady English speaking guy asked if we were looking for girls, and I answered that my friend was lonely and looking for maybe one girl that could help him out. Our new buddy led us to a strip club that didn't look like much outside in the middle of the day but was a paradise behind closed doors. The facility was comfortably dark, lit with the requisite neon lights, had loud Spanish pop music, no other customers, and most importantly was full of strippers that had nothing to do. We were quickly approached by two women, a beautiful young bailarína for me, and a more appropriately matched older dancer for Neckbeard. The veteran stripper spoke English and sized up the situation with impressive speed and accuracy. She asked Neckbeard if he wanted a kiss and when he said yes she gave him one right on the lips. Seeing my plan come to fruition grossed me out more than anything and I immediately felt badly for the woman who was now kissing lips that women of more fortunate circumstance had unanimously passed on. The old pro asked Neckbeard if he wanted to go downstairs with her and when he looked my way for support I sent a nod that conveyed when in Rome do as the Romans. I also implored him to leave an excellent tip.

La Bailarína moved onto my lap and tried to get the point across with giggles and facial expressions. I unloaded some high school level Spanish on her and we chopped through a conversation about our names, ages and favorite animals. She kept breaking my concentration by rubbing my dick through my pants and stirred me to realize she wanted money more than she cared to get to know me and hear me recite all the colors of the wheel. Another stripper stopped by and asked if I wanted to buy La Bailarína a drink. I said sure and handed over some cash, which made change that was returned to me in Mexican currency fanning out around a silver platter with our drinks in the middle. La Bailarína shot her drink quickly and then dragged me toward the downward stairwell that had just engulfed Neckbeard and the new love of his life. I was pretty sure I didn't want to see the bottom of those stairs but La Bailarína was very persuasive and light years more attractive than my girlfriend.

The basement no longer felt like a strip club and was merely a cement room with multiple partitions and curtains for privacy. La Bailarína led me to a scary looking man sitting at a card table with a cash register. He asked straight away if I wanted to fuck her and I declined, knowing I'd still give her money and just save her the indignity of having to have sex with me. I figured she probably had a family, maybe kids already, and this was her best way to make financial contributions. I was also quite certain that the scary looking man took more than his fair share of her income. I handed over some money that went into the cash register, and La Bailarína led me into a private space to watch her dance. She started grooving to music emitted from a simple radio and shed her clothes. She was a young and beautiful Hispanic woman and her body was perfect in every way. She had a youthful face, long and silky black hair, fabulous tits, a glowing ass, and was fit and smooth all over. I was only taken out of the moment once when I saw her underwear was decorated with Micky Mouse, instantly recalling a previously profound encounter with Disney panties. Despite giving her an out, La Bailarína undid my pants and did her best to masturbate me. Riddled with guilt, I tucked my erect penis back in and gave her more money, that when she dressed she hid in her bustier. When the song on the radio ended, I heard Neckbeard awkwardly call out for me from somewhere else in the room.

We headed for the door after having spent all our money which probably didn't amount to much profit for the establishment. I know for sure Neckbeard didn't bring enough cash to actually make touching him worthwhile to a woman. I still feel like our state department needs to issue an apology to that over-thehill burlesque queen. She did say goodbye to Neckbeard, which is more than I got from La Bailarína who rejoined her coworkers as quickly as she could after leaving me. High rollers we were not. Outside, I asked Neckbeard if he got laid and he said he could only afford a blow job. I asked him how it was and he said with no emotion that he came harder than he had ever come in his life. A wave of nausea swept over me but I was a little happy for the fellow. Then, instead of thanking me or living in the moment a little, the asshole asked if on the way home we could stop by a Blockbuster. Neckbeard wanted to rent movies but only from a selection he had already viewed before and he wanted to order a pizza or five. I appealed to him to not post anything about our adventure online then tuned him out as best I could to fantasize about La Bailarína. Neckbeard did a hundred more stupid things while with me and without the benefit of my future mental and behavioral health training, I had no way of knowing this dipshit at minimum was Asperger as fuck.

CHAPTER NINE

Fourth Lover – Delcine (Guatemalan Princess)

The farthest I ever traveled to get laid was 2,207 miles. I was a student at the University of Arizona and found it much harder to make personal connections than it had been at Pima Community College. As a journalism student, my building was a significant distance removed from the rest of the campus and since I had transferred with a lower degree I had no need to take larger core subjects that would have meant meeting more of the student body. The journalism students were mostly dweebs that I couldn't stand. They were the variety of kids to go to the professor during an exam and point out a typo on the test so we'd all have to stop and correct it. I derived schadenfreude like pleasure from wildcat sporting defeats because losses always formed little black clouds above my peers that would float with them for days. I hadn't had a girlfriend in more than two years and wasn't doing much to maintain my platonic friendships either.

I had hated my K through 12 experience but unexpectedly enjoyed community college. Then I circled back to hating life at the university. However, that bump of success in community college kept me motivated to push through to graduation. Instead of lying down, I piled on the summer school courses and aimed to reduce the needed time spent at the University of Arizona. Summer school can seem intimidating until you realize that the scheduled five hour running time for classes never actually lasts that long. The summer school teachers phone it in and give students their credits without much hassle. An advanced Spanish class in particular was surprisingly easy, and a weighty project simply asked us to communicate with Latin America.

I made my pen pal by adding as many hot babes as I could on MySpace. I sent friend requests south of the border and poorly flirted in Spanish with the women who accepted. I set out to be funny and disruptive to the class but actually met some interesting women. Most of these new friends were from Mexico and many of them were also university students. One connection, my same age, was about to graduate as a biologist and continue working to save the sea turtles. She once sent me a sexy picture to show off her tattoos of marine reptiles. Another connection, slightly younger than me, was a party planner in Mexico City who I would meet a decade later when she visited family in Arizona. She would come with an empty suitcase and a fat stack of hundred dollar bills, and I'd help her buy Nintendos and all the electronics asked for by little relatives. All of these women were super classy.

Delcine was the most helpful to my coursework. She lived in Guatemala and worked in the city at an American cellphone company's call center. She spoke English from having watched Friends on TV and was naturally intelligent with no real education. Delcine emailed me literature about Guatemala's civil war, government, and national figures that helped get me an A in summer school. When the class ended and I moved on to other things, she fired off one last email asking where I was and demanded a good reason to not be upset with me. I thought her entitlement was cute and decided to keep talking to her. We exchanged letters and gifts in the mail, and because I lived at home my parents came to know her, too. Which is most likely why they were supportive of sending me to visit.

At least at first my mom and dad were excited about me traveling to Guatemala to visit Delcine. Then my mom received warnings from the state department website that cautioned Americans against Guatemalan travel, especially around the holidays, because the airport was under construction, gang crime was rampant, and the lowest class believed people from the U.S. wanted to steal babies. But I could not be persuaded away from meeting Delcine. She had sent too many bikini photos of herself posing on the black sand beaches of Guatemala, and was way too hot and exotic looking for me to pass up. I remember sitting in Tucson International Airport, watching news break that Gerald Ford had just passed, making plans to keep my money safe by carrying it in an under-the-clothing wallet, and not at all worried about my likely murder.

Landing in Guatemala was a little nerve-racking. As with any Internet introduction, I kept waiting for the moment Delcine and I would first see and react to each other. Typically, some established thoughts about the other person ring true while many others have to fall away as they are revealed to have only made sense in cyberspace. Except the crowd of travelers from my airplane kept being herded between disconnected buildings, as the airport really was under construction and in dangerous disarray. Also, non-fliers are kept out of the airport and the mass of people outside are mostly there to beg for money. Seeing Delcine in the mix was more of a relief than a magic moment because I suddenly had somebody to help evacuate me to safety. I pulled Delcine through a barrier into my part of the terminal and we found the cab she had waiting.

The taxi Delcine called was driven by a friend of her father and she explained that getting into a cab with an unknown driver almost certainly meant she'd be driven off somewhere and raped. Delcine only had time to get me to the Holiday Inn in Guatemala City and then promised she would see me the next day on her lunch break. She lived in a village and worked in the city, so although her home was far from me her office was close and set the stage for how we would spend time together over the next week. When Delcine dropped me off in the hotel lobby I finally got to take a minute and absorb her offline presence. She was exceptionally beautiful with distinctly Mayan features. Delcine was petite and exotic with flowing black hair. She dressed very well and carried herself with class. She had to say goodbye quickly because of her father's friend waiting in the cab but promised to see me in the next afternoon and warned me not to venture through the streets without her.

I woke up the next day and decided to take a walk around Guatemala City. I got myself lost and entirely missed Delcine's first visit. She had sat in the hotel cafe and cried but left me a note saying when she would be back. I had spent the day wandering the streets, baking under the sun, and wondering how long until I got robbed and dismembered. I handed a lot of cash over to the little children that followed me around, only later finding out that I shouldn't because this source of income is what keeps their parents from sending them to school. I wondered why there were so many armed guards in Guatemala because I wasn't used to seeing a uniformed man holding a shotgun outside every grocery store and McDonald's. Although I initially got myself lost to a degree that caused me a great deal of concern, I eventually established my sense of direction and discovered the market, bank and services I would consistently use for the remainder of my trip. I also wandered into a Hooter's Guatemala which cut a nice slice of home.

Delcine and I hit it off when together and made many wonderful memories in Guatemala. We ordered a tour from my hotel which deceptively turned out to be a guy and his van. Although he knew enough to make a few interesting comments about historical places in Guatemala, he was still just a guy and his van. The tour consisted of me, Delcine, and a young Canadian nerd who was also staying in my hotel. It must have been awkward for the Canadian but since I traveled this far to be with a sexy Guatemalan woman I still constantly groped and made out with Delcine. The Canadian would from time to time try and make small talk with us but mostly kept to his third wheel status or tried hanging out with the tour guide. The tour guide, however, would frequently take us somewhere and then disappear with his van for long stretches of time, most likely up to criminal or at least questionable activity. Delcine and I went right on kissing and petting each other, keeping our Canadian friend uncomfortable.

Sleeping with Delcine was awkward because of the hotel's policy to not let young women who were non guests of the hotel go into the rooms. This was apparently to cut down on prostitution paid for by American business travelers. To get Delcine into my room the two times she slept over, we had to surrender our passports and agree to paying a penalty. The fee was worth it as Delcine was a woman who if I had found back home would no doubt pass me over and fall for an entirely different kind of guy. Undressing Delcine was surreal because I hadn't ever been with this caliber of woman. Every piece of clothing was fashionable right down to her purple G-string. The lovemaking was intense and passionate, and the long baths and holding each other that filled the times between sex was also hot and romantic.

In this trip, I did meet Delcine's family. I spent New Year's Eve with them and watched as their countrymen blew up most of the surrounding public property. I found it unsafe to be igniting bombs near power boxes and telephone poles but Delcine laughed it off and said her people lose limbs, go blind, and even kill themselves celebrating every holiday. A volcano erupted in the horizon, and the red lava percolating in the black sky behind the flurry of fireworks made for an emotional night that nicely summed up my time with Delcine in Guatemala. Although her family accepted me, none of them spoke English and her father in particular watched me suspiciously. If I had to put words to the silence between us when he drove me home after the party, I think her dad wanted to ask me why I traveled so far to meet his daughter and what I thought I had to offer her. Meanwhile, Delcine's mom was telling her to go back with me because the U.S. was a more prosperous country and offered more opportunities to young women than could Guatemala.

Delcine's version of the American dream was different than what her mother had hoped for her. Regrettably, I did bring Delcine to the U.S. and I watched her personality change as she went from having nothing to having everything. My parents were going to pay for her education but she avoided classes and watched TV all day. She could somehow enjoy watching a marathon of cooking shows. It didn't matter what she was watching, she just liked broadcasting garbage into her brain and being waited on. When the neighborhood exterminator mistook her for my parents' maid, I laughed it off and told him that she doesn't know where we keep any cleaning supplies. She also liked completing online surveys for money, with each $100 check making her feel like a millionaire. She hoarded coupons and free samples and created towers of waste that depressed everyone around her. I graduated from university with a bachelor's degree that didn't open any doors for me. I took a job in a big box store that was infinitely worse than the grocery store position I held before college. Delcine and I got an apartment together that she trashed, and I counted down the days until immigration services would intervene and send her home. She had been out of compliance with her student visa for a long time, as her grades and attendance were non-existent. Except Delcine would never go back. She was done with Guatemala, though kept telling everyone that she was a Mayan princess who deserved the best in life. She went on to marry a manager from the big box store and moved with him to Phoenix to together run an even bigger iteration of the same nasty retail behemoth. Last I checked, she was in charge of the beauty department which is both vain and appropriate. The free world blackened Delcine's heart, and I regret my part in changing that girl for the worse. Our week together in Guatemala amounted to a beautiful brief romance that we ruined by extending several years.

CHAPTER TEN

Susie and Shanny (The Therapeutic Group Home for Teenage Girls)

Susie and Shanny were both a few years older than me and very beautiful girl-next-door types. Susie had long, curly brown hair and Shanny had short, straight blond hair. As I was right out of college, I'd have been too intimidated to try and get to know either of these women in the wild. But since I met them at work, where people come to know and depend on each other over time, they both took an interest in me that I would not have otherwise gotten to enjoy. Unfortunately, workplace dating is a paradox. I can meet women easily but the relationships are doomed to fail. At some point, everybody learns this lesson.

My journalism degree from the University of Arizona opened no doors for me. I worked in a grocery store before college and then after college succumbed to working in a big box warehouse. The new job was infinitely worse than the old job, which provoked me to start solving problems on my own rather than keep on believing things people told me, like college being a worthwhile venture. Since I spent my nights stocking the electronics and entertainment department in a soulless corporate hellhole, I browsed Craigslist for other graveyard shifts that might be less physically demanding. Or with fewer homophobic tirades launched at me from the night supervisor who thought I'd unpack the DVD new releases faster if I knew the consequence was him gay raping me. Eventually I applied at a therapeutic group home for teenage girls because the only requirements given in the ad were the ability to stay up late and clean toilets. I formed an alliance with a team leader in the big box warehouse who was going to pose as my supervisor in exchange for me writing him a reference letter about his skillful leadership that he could likewise use to find better employment. I rolled the dice and quit my job before the next one was offered to me and it all worked out in the end.

When the group home hired me, I was for lack of any relevant experience picturing a hospital setting. When my training began, which took place in daytime at the boys' home, I was wholly unprepared for a little kid to come barreling out of what looked like a normal house with a PlayStation tucked under his arm. Unexpectedly, the angry youngster hurled the machine at a cactus and when it exploded, looked at me like a thug and asked what I thought about that. He added that I was a bitch before nonchalantly walking back inside. Confused, worried and curious, I picked up the broken electronic pieces and entered the facility where I was greeted by another young boy who casually asked if I could put the game console back together. Looking around, I saw a group of children and teens who were all disheveled, bored, and in some cases wrestling with each other around the brick fireplace and broken furniture. Now I just wondered who the hell was watching these hooligans, and the answer over time was that nobody really watches them. When my first shift of night training came around, I was asked to shadow a senior staff who was a college faring young man others thought kept to himself and did homework all night. Despite no experience in the field whatsoever, it took me all of 30 minutes to realize loner guy was beyond inappropriate with the girls. I took my findings to the clinical director and when she saw that this pervert also added the underage residents as friends on his social media he was promptly fired and reported to authorities. My reward was now being the only overnight male staff alone in a house full of teenage girls savvy enough to make false accusations. I was terrified.

Except the girls never hurt me. I treated the residents with respect and they answered by making my life easy. The day shift and the residents were often times at war with each other during waking hours and then both sides always felt relieved when I came on duty. I'd send the girls to bed with a wink and then let them back out when the day workers finished their final paperwork and left. The set bedtime was way too early for teens and if I let them come out to watch a movie and have some snacks then they would go to bed a second time, more reasonably tired and without a battle. I also asked the girls to never go AWOL on me and always make choices that wouldn't jeopardize my job, and I can't think of a time a resident put me in a bad position with the site supervisor or clinical director. In fact, since most overnight workers had been lazy misfits that watched TV and slept all night without ever picking up a mop or a broom, I only had to do the bare minimum cleaning to be hailed as the best ever hired for the home. I was sympathetic to the girls living under our roof, and always gave them time and attention when they woke up at night and told me they were sad or lonely. Sometimes it was an act to be out of their rooms but more often than not it was the truth and I didn't mind breaking the rules to be decent to another human being. Besides, I could clean that entire house in an hour and spend the rest of the night dicking around on the Internet. Life was smooth sailing and I happily floated a year away from working in the retail giant. I've said it before and it's still true, the young people I'm supposed to help in these human service jobs always do more for me than I do for them.

The employees, on the other hand, are a necessary stupidity. The problem is anybody can get a job in a group home because the work is low paid and has high turnover. I was satisfied working the night shift half of the week opposite an obese woman who worked the other half. She was chair ridden and the house was disgusting when I took over but I liked her, we were friends, and the extra work she made for me by not cleaning didn't amount to more than it would take to faze me and my overall happiness. Meanwhile, our coworkers from the day slots were always unhappy over the grueling hours of managing every resident's schedule of school, therapy and probation, and always quitting over every girl's teenage fangs, venomous attitude, and dehumanizing bites. The girls were very experienced character assassins and could root out a grown person's insecurities and attack with the most draining insults, like how this staff is fat, lonely and unloved, and this other staff is a cowardly, sycophantic nark who sucks up to bosses. One time, a happy go lucky recent college grad thinking she was going to segue group home experience into psychology work came into the house for her training, was told by a teenage girl that her murder was imminent, got back in her car and left just as abruptly. Of all the faceless workers who rotated through those daytime jobs, the two who stood out were Susie and Shanny.

Susie and Shanny weren't particularly good at their jobs, and again I was saved by the mutual respect shared between me and the teenage girls we all supported. I'd frequently find that the day shift left knives that were supposed to be locked when not in use submerged in sink water after dinner and other dangers that could have been exploited by residents had they wished to rise against me. I don't know as much about Shanny but Susie herself grew up in a group home and didn't know what to do as an adult besides work in one. She was scatterbrained and comfortable rushing into work late on her mornings, which kept me on shift longer, so she could shower, blow dry, dress and apply makeup in the girls' bathroom. I had to work for free when the day shift kept me over because reporting my real hours would clue the site supervisor and clinical director into who wasn't coming to work on time. Susie thought she could make up for my wasted time by sending me pictures of her ass and tits. I wasn't working long before attending a team meeting where Susie sent me a text message complaining that she'd rather be sucking my dick than listening to the site supervisor. Another time, I came to work to find the day shift scrambling to come up with a search and rescue plan over some girls that ran away, and again Susie pushed a private parallel plan at me whereby we'd volunteer to search the neighborhood with the 15 passenger van but instead park somewhere and fuck. I enjoyed the attention but never took Susie up on her offers, creating a professional rule of thumb that dictated I not do anything on the job that would if caught make a salacious headline for Fox News. Susie showed up in the middle of the night one lonely shift having prepared an extravagant seafood dinner complete with breadsticks and drinks. I couldn't help but make out with and grind on her but stopped short of fucking her in the group home, deterring myself by writing the news in my head: Sexual Deviants Fired From Teen House.

So where does Shanny fit in? Susie felt rejected by me and started chipping away at my blissful routine by using the girls and my tacit friendship with them to create friction between me and the day shift. Suddenly, I wasn't a team player and my way of doing things jeopardized the overall discipline strategy of the home (there wasn't one). In my infinite wisdom, I decided the best way to fight back was to seduce Susie's best friend at work, Shanny. I asked Shanny to hang out and she accepted, setting in motion a friendship where Shanny and I frequently got together before my night shift on her days off and after her day shift on my nights off. I accomplished my goal of stroking Susie's anger which predictably made my situation one hundred times worse, leaving me unsure as to my original hope for this strategy. When shenanigans got so out of hand that the site supervisor and clinical director dropped the hammer on all of us, Susie and Shanny got together and quit. They both sweetly approached me the next week and asked me to serve as a reference on standby in their new job searches. Shanny sent me some nice postcards in the mail as she traveled and moved away, and Susie came full circle back to sending me dirty texts. What I walked away having learned besides my hidden passion for disenfranchised teens, is that work environments are micro dating ecosystems where people feel like they know each other and can approach each other for relationships with minimum risk despite the long term negative consequences staring everybody in the face, and that whenever I screw around with women on the job they will always suffer for it more than I do.

I probably should have fucked Susie in the van.

CHAPTER ELEVEN

Sixth Lover – Faith (Married Coworker)

Love, lust and attraction are all powerful and interesting feelings. Not all of the women I've been with came neatly one right after the other. Some of them overlapped and even impacted each other's interactions with me. Faith was another coworker of mine in the mental and behavioral health company whose calm and perky demeanor infuriated the loose cannon that was my primary and bipolar love interest. While caught in the protracted hell that was my on and off again relationship, Faith threw a party at her home and invited me. Even though my insanely religious lover and I were off at the time, the siren still forbade me from going to Faith's social gathering. She even used her Christian mouth to dub Faith a fucking little work princess. And so being banned from the party meant I was going for sure. Normally, I would have stayed home and never known that Faith was looking to have an extramarital affair with me. Thanks, bipolar!

I didn't set out to become the office slut but destiny has a way of choosing us while we are on the path we take to avoid it. I did find Faith attractive the first time I saw her. She joined the clinic after having been a preschool teacher and was going to perform as a family aide, which meant she was going to support service plans by teaching simple life skills to children with behavior challenges. A family aide is considered a lowly skilled staff and of course cheaper than a master's level therapist but often times proven immeasurably more valuable. Family aides tended to not have enormous egos and were able to build up natural relationships with angry and underperforming kids. Therapists usually thought too highly of themselves and were always dreaming up asinine groups like drum circle that only made kids angrier and more disruptive. Faith was a caring family aide and recommended to me by the family support director for many of the children whose cases I managed. From talking to Faith on the phone, I knew she was young and from Texas. Her accent gave away that she was going to be smoking hot.

I met Faith in person for the first time in the home of one of my few clients that was with a legitimate mental handicap. A child in this position normally needed a state worker who could prescribe services designed to last a lifetime. These workers responded slowly as the state is even more inept than the network of mental and behavioral health providers, and so often times I would just meet with these families and do what I could for them. I obviously couldn't cure mental retardation but I could maybe offer some life skills to the client or show the family new techniques for teaching hygiene and self care. Faith brought a positive attitude into this particular home and left her mark by increasing this child's dignity. Faith asked that the child be dressed properly for sessions and told the mom it was unacceptable for him to spend all of his time in underwear. Unlike the female in my ongoing workplace romance, Faith was actually effective and not an uncaring fraud.

Faith was indeed from Texas and married. Her husband was said to make good money and she lived in a nice house with him. They had no children and no need for Faith to work. Faith got to choose what to do with her time and wanted to continue helping kids in need. Faith was very attractive and took excellent care of herself. She was young, her skin was milky smooth, and she never had a long brown hair out of place. She mostly wore cute dresses, and she decorated her office space with hearts and everything pink. She was liked by everyone except my bitter bipolar girlfriend. Faith took a liking to me because as a case manager I stayed directly involved with the children and their assigned supports. I was the only case manager that gave up weekends to take kids on fun field trips, or spent the daytime hours performing as an extra family aide, which pushed my paperwork back for me to do over the night. If a child's behavioral goal needed more attention than normal, I often times scheduled myself as a backup family aide to add that many more sessions into a client's time with us. While most family aides aspire to become case managers, I eventually tired of doing the case management work at night and just accepted that I was happier as a family aide. Faith's affection for me grew as together we helped guide and encourage more children to be successful in their lives.

Faith squealed with delight when I got to her party. Her and her husband's home was filled with our coworkers who were barbequing, drinking, swimming and playing frat kind of games together. Faith was in a bikini and wasted no time leading me by hand into the bathroom of her master bedroom. She slid the two triangle pieces of her bikini to each side and in one smooth motion had freed a perfect pair of tits. I had no time to take in her boobs as she threw herself into me and stole an apparently long overdue kiss. I couldn't believe how giddy she was to be making out with me. My head was spinning until Faith spun me around, recovered herself, and took me by hand back out to the party. Faith insisted I disrobe enough to get in the hot tub with her and we joined some curious coworkers. Everyone knew Faith was married and thought it a little strange that this party was happening while her husband was away on business. Not having paid attention to much other than my crazy girlfriend, I was unaware of the party's backstory.

Faith was visibly drunk and a few of the more responsible coworkers started asking her to slow down. She scoffed at them and stayed close to me in the hot tub. Eventually, when somebody questioned her drunkenness she moved herself to my lap, straddled me face to face, and planted sloppy kisses on my lips in front of everyone. Some of the women gasped and plenty of the guys applauded. Faith whispered to me that she didn't want to leave her husband, suspected that I didn't want to leave the bipolar chick, and suggested we just go into her bedroom and fuck each other. I couldn't find any fault in her logic so that's what we did. After we fucked, she cried just like the woman before her and similarly told me that her husband doesn't look at her and she just wants to feel desirable and worthy. I tucked her in and told her that she has more options now at her young age than if she waits any more years to leave him. She drifted off to sleep knowing she wasn't going to make any changes.

I felt guilty because my heart belonged to my other coworker so I drove from the party to her apartment and fucked her, too. I had shown up at the door and told her only that I made out with another woman and that she needed to decide if we were going to be together or not. She flipped her lid and illogically demanded I go buy a toothbrush and come back. When I returned, she watched me brush my teeth twice, made me do it again, and then we reconciled with steamy sex. Obviously all hell was going to break loose in the next few days but I was happy that for the moment I had my codependent lover back. I don't know why she had such a hold over me but she was my drug.

Back at work, I had forgotten that my actions didn't occur in a vacuum. I was checking out a chart when the young guy working behind the medical records counter called me a home wrecker and then offered a cheeky high five. Shit.

CHAPTER TWELVE

Seventh Lover – Guinevere (English Professor)

Without the Internet, the number of women I've had in my life drastically dwindles to just a lonely handful. I wonder if living in an offline day and age, relying on my own raw ability out of necessity, would have made a difference in my pursuit of a rewarding relationship experience. Meeting women online is as easy as dragging girls I like into a virtual shopping cart and clicking checkout. I quickly learned the online dating tricks that guaranteed as many dates as I could possibly want, and developed routines to build attraction and intimacy that worked almost every time. Unfortunately, this practice resulted in quantity over quality.

The first time I filled out a dating profile was when I challenged myself to not dwell on the psychotic coworker I couldn't fuck anymore thanks to HR drawing up a map that kept us separated for the rest of our careers. I foolishly went about my registration as if writing an honest profile would deliver the intended results. Knowing what I know now, the best male profile is brief and ignores most of the more time consuming content, has just a couple photos, and cautions that most women aren't going to make the cut. This nets the maximum attention from women and receives the most unsolicited messages. Women want to go on dates with good looking men and minimize the time spent reading boring life summaries and repeating cookie cutter conversations.

My first profile where I uploaded as many photos as possible and droned on about myself in five paragraph essays immediately received a message which gave me a false sense of what this experience was going to be like. Ultimately, online dating for me unfolded like some of those popular role playing games I tried to get into on my Gameboy but came to hate. In those, I'm happy enough while making my character, taking a few steps, encountering a monster and defeating it, getting rewarded, feeling positively reinforced until the same thing happens a maddening thousand more times and I only keep going because I'm convinced the real payoff must come after just one more exercise in futility. The first message I received was from a University of Arizona professor named Guinevere and all she asked in an incomplete and unpunctuated question was if I was interested.

I asked Guinevere to clarify what I might be interested in and she answered that if I were not a serial killer then she was wondering if I wanted to have some fun with her. She appeared fit and attractive and had written some interesting things on her profile such as her to do list for Arizona. Guinevere had come from an out of state college and was now a PhD candidate in Literature and Film claiming to have an interest in exploring the tourist traps and desert culture. She told me that she had cinema passes and suggested we begin with a traditional dinner and movie date. I agreed and she asked me what I wanted to see. I told her I hadn't seen Captain America and she groaned that she usually doesn't see such lowly fare but it had been so long since she went to the movies she may just appreciate the experience. Guinevere was my first but not last egomaniac, and women in academics who thought too highly of themselves became my most common online dating partner archetype. I'm proud to have saved many students a load of stress by fucking their teachers late at night after the teachers teased that they really should be writing harder exam questions.

En route to my first Internet arranged soiree, I got the ritualistic text message from my date confirming that she was also on her way. As every date goes, I saw Guinevere sitting down swiping through her phone and I observed that she more or less looked like her pictures. Guinevere stood up and offered her hand and said it was nice to meet me and wanted to know if this restaurant was still OK. Our dinner was in the mall, as was the theater, so we sat down and she showed me that she had printed our tickets to Captain America. She still made it seem like lowering herself to my level was an act for which I needed to show thanks. Hey, don't do me or Steve Rogers any favors. We then proceeded to have a really lame conversation about our lives.

Guinevere ordered strange food seemingly choosing what was different over what might actually taste good, and told me that she was still married but in the final stages of divorce (another archetype). She bragged about being in Mensa and said this is also where she met her husband who is more than 30 years her senior. Guinevere described one idiotic life decision after another. She said the man that got her pregnant also beat her up. A romantic relationship with the older man from the IQ society grew solely from their highbrow email exchanges. They wed and he adopted her son. Now that they are divorcing she expects child support from the wealthy sexagenarian and now legal father of her son. His child support payments also give him long visitation rights. Guinevere then ranted that her ex husband to be is a sociopath with no real emotions. Horrified, I couldn't figure out why she would want money from a man she despises if it means her son would have to go live with him each summer. How does somebody screw up their life so badly and still think so highly of themselves? Guinevere also enjoyed dropping author names into the conversation knowing I had no idea what literature she was referencing. The dinner was so awkward and painful that I thought skipping the movie and calling it a night was a no brainer.

As I uncomfortably stirred my ice, Guinevere decided it was time to go sit for Captain America. I was surprised that we were going through with this but really wanted to see the movie. As we walked from the restaurant to the theater entrance, I reflected on her actually being quite cute. She wore a hippie style of a blouse and skirt that fit her shapely body well and she paired her outfit with adorable sneakers. I kinda dug her look. She looked flirty and fun and at least the talking part of the date was mostly over. If

Guinevere was the kind of woman that Internet dating had to offer then I still anticipated good things to come. I would also learn that the uncomfortable nonsense I just went through isn't even that important. From my perspective, I wrongly assumed that dates want to get to know me as a person. Future dates worked better when I skipped the part where the women and I interview each other.

Our film was a few weeks into its run so we were practically alone in the auditorium. Guinevere rested her head on my shoulder for a second before any previews rolled only to pop back up and ask if I kiss on the first date. Trying to figure out how I misread the first half of our evening, I told her I wasn't opposed to kissing her. She reasoned that was a yes and then leaned in for some making out. I commented that the date had suddenly improved and she assured me that it would get better yet. The movie entertained us and Guinevere just minimally injected her analytical commentary. Her assertions of intellectual superiority became less obnoxious to me after she made her body accessible. We walked outside and of course her little car was ruined by a comical number of wonky liberal bumper stickers. As Guinevere and I made out in the parking lot she kept provoking me to be more aggressive. I'd stop to let a family walk by without us making them uncomfortable and she'd loudly ask why I wasn't interested in touching more of her body. She announced that she was wearing black panties and rolled the top of her skirt down for me to see the ruffled waistband of an expensive brand. I put a little more effort into my part of this tango and pushed her against her car, kissed her harder, and grabbed a boob and a butt cheek. Yep, that's what she wanted. Guinevere explained that she had a babysitter at home she needed to relieve but if I went to her apartment about an hour later the next night then her son would be asleep. Was this an invitation to fuck already? She then added that she was expecting her period but would still get me off. Okie dokie.

Guinevere answered her door the next night and informed me that her son was still awake. She brought me inside anyway and introduced me as mommy's friend. She ordered him to brush his teeth and he disappeared into a bathroom. Guinevere's apartment was nicely furnished and to her credit she played the part of a liberal academic. She had a library with stacked shelves of books that reached the ceiling, and she went around gathering texts for me to take home. Whatever. I figured I could drive her books around in my trunk for awhile and then return them. Her son came back and wanted us to verify his mouth was clean. Guinevere told her boy to shut his door and go to bed quickly. She let me know that we would wait about ten minutes for him to actually be asleep. I felt like a creeper because of the innocent child's dad problems but still asked Guinevere how this was supposed to work. She answered that it works just like this and slipped out of her clothes. She invited me into her bed and asked that I excuse the alarming number of dildos she needed to collect from the sheets and stow in a drawer. Then Guinevere slid over to my side of the bed, put her hand on my crotch, and said I was about to get my dick sucked.

Guinevere gave me the best blow job of my life. She described what she was going to do before she started and said I was in store for lots of teasing, a big build up, and a great explosion of pleasure delivered by her mouth. She made good on every claim and after swallowing my cum exhaled a proud breath as if she had just refreshed herself in a delicious soft drink commercial. She told me she loves giving head but her husband was never interested. She put on a movie she liked and reverted back to telling me why the director picked his color saturation. Guinevere informed me that spending the night or not was optional but I could come back in a few days for sex. I did not spend the night but I came back after her period for sex. Guinevere and I had intercourse which she enjoyed less than sucking my dick, and told me it takes a powerful phallic toy to get her off. In my mind, I told her that she also doesn't inspire as much passion or effort as my true love who was in exile just beyond the workplace restraining order.

I soon asked Guinevere what we were doing and she truthfully said she intended to play the field until she found her romantic and intellectual match which she clearly thought I was not. She said her marriage cooped her up and she wanted to flex her freedom by having a fling and slumming with some dumb stud. She said she picked me for her first foray into the gutter because I looked and sounded like she could get away with it. We agreed to stay loosely connected and both took turns in the future helping the other out when an event came up where we wanted to arrive with a date. She was a much better fake date than a real date. When I needed her, she acted like an attached floozie in front of my astonished coworkers and scored me some cool points. Guinevere was never a woman with whom I wanted to be in a serious relationship. I searched for her online and saw gross wedding photos of her feeding cake to a 60 year old man, I laughed at spiteful rants her students left on those rate-my-educator websites, and I was turned off by her personal homepage erected to her academic accomplishments. Still, she gave me an amazing blow job and unexpected compliment. I'm a dumb stud that women want to frivolously fuck and discard on their journey to happiness? I wish someone told me sooner.

God bless America.

CHAPTER THIRTEEN

Eighth Lover – Harmony (Art Teacher)

Harmony is the most conventionally attractive woman of which I have had a sexual relationship. She isn't the most beautiful to me but if she and my other lovers were lined up and society were asked to select the hottest then I must concede she would win. She was my only blonde. She acted quickly to have sex with me and removed herself from my life just as fast. There were steps I could have taken with the benefit of more experience to keep her interested for longer but ultimately I can't keep a woman like Harmony nor am I interested in doing so.

While Internet dating, I had a strong sense of who to message. I quickly became aware of my range and knew that initiating conversations with women beyond my scope was a waste of time. Harmony sat on the upper edge of attractive women that might write back when I shot her a message that cut to the chase and asked for a date. She accepted and provided her phone number. We exchanged the minimum amount of texting necessary to arrange a coffee date and she suggested a trendy place near the University of Arizona where she lived and went to school. She demonstrated enthusiasm throughout this process.

In hot girl fashion, Harmony pushed our date hours and hours back until it seemed ridiculous for me to even see it through but, in overly excited man fashion, I dutifully waited for her to get her shit together. The coffee shop was one of those eyesores where hipsters carve their idiotic ravings on the wall, and signs have to be posted reminding freeloaders on the WiFi to purchase something at least once every two hours. As I Internet dated, I became familiar with these places and recycled them for more dates. A woman might introduce me to her dive of a hangout before dumping me and then I'd suggest it to her replacement like I'd been going there with gusto for years. Harmony finally came in and, as if making me wait wasn't insulting enough, stood in line to purchase her drink before acknowledging me. C'mon, I was only a few feet away!

Our date was brief because apparently a friend was having a crisis and Harmony was going to have to go involve herself in some nonsense blah blah blah. Harmony made my head spin, wanted me to take the second sip right out of her cup, and acted like we were old friends. She suggested that if I were still around after she tended to her emergency then we could meet up again and resume our date but, since I didn't know what I'd do besides wander around empty parks and probably encounter a scary homeless person, I just asked if we might see each other on another night. Harmony agreed to date number two and we walked to our cars which were conveniently parked next to each other. She hugged me tightly and scurried off to do whatever the hell a hot girl does for a friend suddenly having a problem after midnight.

I thought about Harmony and all I had learned was that she was an art student, aspired to work in a high school after graduation, and had a toddler son who she bestowed with a weird ass ancient name she thought meant journey to the stars or something absurd. I never met the kid but I assured myself that with a teaspoon of intelligence he would be able to chop off enough syllables to make a less humiliating nickname. Harmony's baby daddy was in the Border Patrol and she had to drive over two hours twice a week to share custody. It would turn out that a lot of my dates had hooked up with the Border Patrol and all of their experiences were overwhelmingly negative. Harmony's erratic personality and distracted focus should have been red flags but she was a stunningly beautiful woman eight years younger than me so of course I wanted to see her again. I ignored that she liked to affectionately refer to her smartphone as the little faggot.

Harmony planned our second date to predictably disastrous results. She had these hole in the wall obscurities in her memory that now either no longer existed or were since condemned by the health department. We drove around and finally settled on a foreign place she noticed because she thought she liked that kind of food. The service was slow and the meal was icky but we managed to keep a conversation going and I was encouraged by her having asked me to pick her up and provide this date's transportation. I get asked by so many dates if I am a serial killer that by default I attempt to build confidence by never offering to pick anyone up close to where they live. Harmony didn't perceive me as a threat and even invited me into her home after our experimental dinner. She wanted to switch out clothing she was wearing and then walk to a bar near her student housing. While in her home those passing minutes, she introduced me to her original artwork which was primarily this sty of pigs she sculpted then stuck with syringes, leaving the needles sticking out every which way. She said the concept was an expression about a health condition she suffered through. Huh.

Date two resolved without anything happening except me asking if I could plan date three. Harmony agreed and I picked her up another night, this time with solid traditional plans. I took Harmony to a better restaurant and a casino, and I had cash on hand for us to gamble away. Harmony had two looks and I couldn't decide which was sexier. Actually, whichever one she wore was the sexiest look. She would either straighten her flowing golden hair or curl it and was more beautiful either way. Having her at the casino made me feel like James Bond. She wanted to play table games and the dealers would make a big deal about her and offer her cards or dice to blow on to make lucky. When I got her drinks at the bar, I would overhear men admiring her with their friends. We won money which I let her keep though she did somewhat protest before promising to spend the winnings in a way that included me. All in all, I pulled it off and this hot girl seemed hooked. When I returned her to her doorstep, and hesitated from the sheer hotness intimidation factor, she helped me along and asked if there wasn't anything I was forgetting. I kissed her and she escalated our embrace to full on making out. She exclaimed that she had been waiting the entire night for me to make a move, was slightly offended that I hadn't, and also wondered why I missed so many opportunities on our second date. This was the first time I realized I could attract gorgeous young women, and the moment I fully got over my psychotic coworker.

I invited Harmony over to my apartment for date number four and she was uncharacteristically punctual. I had emailed her a menu from Asian takeout near me and retrieved her desired Thai food before she arrived. I had also purchased an indy film she thought was going to be good but like her choice in food it wasn't. After a halfhearted attempt at viewing her movie she suggested we watch something lighter on my streaming service. I informed her that we needed to move to my bedroom because the on demand content looked better on my computer screen. She may have interpreted that as a come on and it may have worked to my advantage but I was just being honest. We watched one episode of one show and before I could start the next she sat on my lap and rhetorically asked with frustration why I was still taking so long. She took off her top and I obediently collapsed my futon into a bed.

With Harmony, I learned that attractive girls can become offended if you don't try and sleep with them so if you want to there's really no point in waiting. After a short time making love to Harmony without foreplay, she had more curious questions like why I hadn't yet achieved orgasm. She informed me that she already finished several times which I thought was doubtful. She said she had an idea and started sucking my dick but she did so poorly and then stopped, telling me her jaw was once wired shut which limits how tightly she can close her mouth. Her disclosure was my final clue to this medical mystery I couldn't solve. Pork with needles... I just don't get it. Eventually, just by having sex for an appropriate amount of time I ejaculated and she was satisfied. We cuddled up and went to sleep. I woke up first and admired the hot woman I had in my bed but Harmony's luster had diminished ever so slightly in that she was disheveled with smeared makeup, messy hair, and humorously had one tit uncovered. Again, I was learning that there is no reason to go into shock just because a girl is hot – we're all just people. I was also turned off by the coincidence of her having my dad's first name tattooed on her side as if the letters were floating in a bowl of alphabet soup.

Harmony woke up and chided me one last time for taking four whole dates to penetrate her. At this point, I was rolling my eyes at her entitlement. Being a sexy blonde isn't a fast pass to my penis. In fact, I don't even like blondes! Get out. Still, I wanted to keep things going because I knew nothing would do more for my status than dating Harmony. Except Harmony disappeared and I only heard from her once more. After I had fully moved on, she sent me a breakup letter through the dating website as if I had been pining away for her this entire time. She apologized for being distant, informed me that she met somebody with serious potential, and that she assumed I wasn't ever going to fully open up to her anyway. Gibberish. I would have rather known how the cliffhanger ended by her revealing why she was stabbing those swine. By the time I was mostly counseling teenage boys through my job at the mental and behavioral health company, I wandered into a high school and saw Harmony's name listed with the faculty. Good on her for achieving her dream. And when an underachieving senior from my caseload was downtrodden about his life prospects, I told him that at the bare minimum he could join the Border Patrol and come back to fuck his quirky art teacher.

CHAPTER FOURTEEN

Ninth Lover – Isabella (Middle East Professor)

As a professional Internet dater, I had started walking into dates hoping that the woman would be interesting and worthwhile enough for me and not the other way around. Isabella was a sweet young woman who took the initiative in contacting me, and wrote a really nice email as if she had read some of the same coaching websites I did in the beginning. She introduced herself, referenced something I said on my profile, and then gave reasons why she thought I might like her. She latched onto my claim that I was worldly, and shared some of the master's level work she finished over the summer in the middle east for its oppressed LGBT community. Really, I only said I was worldly because I got laid south of the border. However, I liked Isabella's straightforward approach and wanted to reward her confidence with a single date followed by an insincere offer of friendship. My ego was bloated from some perceived early successes with attractive women and I judged Isabella's looks a little harshly. I would realize too late that her value – and sex appeal – ranked way above a pity date.

Isabella picked a cafe that was close to the University of Arizona where she lived, went to school, and had begun teaching some middle eastern language and history to undergrads. She also needed to stay within a certain distance that was accessible to her by bicycle. Her looks and knowing that her only mode of transportation was two wheels left me dismissive of her before we even met. Then she walked into the cafe, still adorably wearing her helmet, and was pleasantly a couple notches cuter than what her pictures had led me to think. She was on the shorter and curvier side but with an exotic turn I liked and uniquely dyed hair that was deep red and almost purple. She dressed well, too. By now I caught myself acting like one of the vain women I had met, as if we're so good looking our dates are jesters in our court and if they don't titillate us we'll wave them away. I quickly adjusted my attitude and intended to take Isabella more seriously. She still seemed bursting with enthusiasm.

Isabella turned out to be a really good date, and figuratively drove everything good that happened to us that night. In our first venue, which was the cafe, she immediately announced that she was hungry from having pedaled all over campus and told me she was going to have to order food. She then gobbled up a vegan sandwich in front of me. That was kind of a turn on since I know a lot of women won't scarf something in front of a man they want to impress, especially if he isn't eating with them. For our second venue, not knowing I was even in store for a location change, Isabella suggested a bar down the street. We went to the billiards establishment with intentions to play pool but never made it past the drink counter because our conversation was so engaging. She had really been in the thick of conflict in the middle east, way more so than any students from my journalism college. Isabella oddly identified as gay even though she preferred to be with men. She claimed to have some ex girlfriends but didn't like the label bisexual since she believed some women say that's what they are just to attract men. Her research in the middle east sounded exciting, dangerous and relevant to humanity. Noticing that our date was going well, Isabella then recommended our third venue. She really read the situation and made suggestions like a man would do under traditional circumstances.

Still in the same night, Isabella took me to a hookah lounge on her dime. Such a place never interested me and I still don't quite know why it exists but apparently a hookah lounge is meaningful to the middle eastern people in Isabella's body of work and she wanted to expose me to some of this culture she loved so much. I became somewhat uncomfortable in here because of how very comfortable the regular hookah enthusiasts were to enter my personal space and make like I needed a new best friend. Isabella enjoyed sharing hookah and banter with strangers but I mostly avoided putting my mouth on anything that was passed my way. As Isabella and our new companions achieved whatever effect comes from hookah, I did the same with good ol' alcohol and eventually planted a well received kiss on Isabella's lips. After we made out some, Isabella glowed brightly and thanked me for making a move, explaining that she was shy and nervous about trying to kiss me later if I didn't kiss her first. I thought her confession was endearing and was flattered to hear that the prospect of kissing me had given her some butterflies.

We finished our night by walking back to the cafe to reunite Isabella and her bicycle. She then, still correctly reading the situation and advancing our date, asked if I wanted to walk a few blocks more with her to see her home safely. We made out on her porch with a little more passion and she over shared her concern that I wouldn't respect her if she invited me to spend the night on our first date. She then reasoned that she also wasn't comfortable not establishing when we would see each other again, and invited me back the next night to watch movies on her laptop. I couldn't tell what the difference would be between having sex on the first date versus making plans to see each other again in fewer than 24 hours specifically to have sex on the second date but enjoyed that Isabella was working hard to win me over. I was truly flattered to know she had been on a mission to make a memorable date and was executing an agenda to bring us closer together. Isabella was a special woman, and her overall attractiveness put her higher than possibly all the women I met Internet dating. I walked back to the cafe from Isabella's porch, smiling until I realized I was alone in a neighborhood where people get shot.

I packed an overnight bag and went to Isabella's home for our second date. She lived with an international student in a little house with two tiny bedrooms that share a bathroom. The roommate was of course a knockout with a sultry accent which didn't bode well for my attraction to my date but I still found Isabella appealing. She was wearing sweatpants and a tank top and although she had more padding than my last few dates she was definitely proportional and ranked slightly above average in desirability. When the roommate finished with the requisite polite appearance and nod to our planned evening she then retired to her room with her dinner, laptop and some homework. Isabella offered me an array of vegetarian snacks she prepared on a platter for us and showed me which movies she had queued on her portable hard drive. Isabella seemed more capable of relaxing and enjoying a night in than me, as I didn't want to pollute my freshly brushed teeth and mouth while she had no problem kissing me with guacamole breath and leaving little bits of chips on my tongue.

I appreciated the trouble Isabella went to putting together the opening ceremony with the finger foods and turning her student laptop into a movie theater but was glad to move past all of it. When she asked if I wanted to join her in the bedroom, I commented that it did feel like we had unfinished business from her porch last night. She led me into her cute and clean room and fucked the shit out of me. I was surprised that I could be made to feel like a lamb ensnared by a lion's overwhelming predation. She stripped me naked before she took her clothes off, and then even though I was on top she grabbed her headboard and intensified the sex by creating tsunamis that rolled across her mattress. She moaned unbelievably filthy language that turned me on though I was never unaware that her innocent roommate and the ability to do homework was caught in this sex storm. When I took a break, I found that the poor foreign girl's door to the shared bathroom was open and she had been happily sitting at her desk with headphones on. I had been fucked too good to react with embarrassment so I held eye contact with the roommate while I walked across the bathroom and shut her door with a smile. Isabella said not to worry and just expect to get used to having sex with someone else around. Isabella then invited me into the shower where she carefully washed my genitals.

Isabella continued introducing me to new things and took me to some middle eastern restaurants, her college office after dark, one of her dance classes, and a swing dance in the warehouse district. Isabella turned out to be very popular, wildly social, and able to cover a lot of ground by bicycle. A cop even wrote her a ticket once for the unsafe manner she had apparently ridden her bike that day. Isabella's interest in me only climbed, though she did catch on to some of my shortcomings. She once asked where the heck were my friends or did I not have any. I did have friends and they were great people, I just hadn't thought about how long I had left them sitting on the back burner while I pursued loose women on the Internet. Dating organically requires a man to water his social garden with friends and hobbies but I was spending that time picking the low hanging fruit online. Isabella claimed that I was the first guy she messaged when she came back from the middle east and that she had only created her account on a lark because she didn't want to be romantically lonely on her approaching birthday. She said I was a better than expected match and that she had disabled her account. Isabella continued trying to please me, and always fucked the shit out of me.

As a professional Internet dater, I decided to invoke the loophole that I could continue pursuing new women because Isabella hadn't explicitly asked me if I had wanted to end my involvement in the website and start an exclusive relationship. Everybody dating online is vulnerable to hearing that they need to step aside for the object of their affection's next challenge, and everybody at some point looks at what they have and thinks that they can do better. The sea is so full it becomes a feeding frenzy of daters chasing the next floating morsel, thinking every bite not yet chomped might make a more perfect meal. The distraction floating before me arrived in a message that simply said hi and nothing else. Clicking through this brief email led to a woman's profile that was scantly filled out but illustrated with jarringly salacious photos. This woman who sent me a single word greeting was young and in incredible shape. One of her pictures was a closeup of her ass in yoga pants with a caption boasting that hard work pays off. Another photo was a closeup of her bust with a caption teasing that buying her a drink might pay off, too. I messaged this new woman for a date and she promptly sent back her phone number. Isabella was about to turn my same age and assumed we would do something together to celebrate her birthday. I knew that any form of participation in her birthday, from just dropping by a party to taking her out one-on-one, would further cement our coupling in her mind and cause more pain for her if our relationship ultimately didn't work out. So I put that thought on the back burner with my unmaintained friendships, and went to meet this vapid girl who posted all the exposed flesh. This girl turned out to be the human iteration of a female praying mantis.

The Mantis had a to-die-for body that was flawless, toned, tanned, tall and on display. Her outfit was basically yoga pants and a bra. Her hair was kept up in dreadlocks that made her look like a sexy villain from a spy movie. I took her on my tried and true casino date but we ran out of money too quickly and we didn't attract the same fun and attention that I had enjoyed on my last gambling outing. I think the difference was the last woman I took to the casino commanded attention by being passively elegant while my new casino date begged for attention by being actively trashy. The Mantis had spent the night telling me about her tough lot in life, having been screwed out of an education (not making grades), screwed out of a good job (not showing up), and all these screwings (not being nice to people) that left her living at home without money and all the luxuries she thought she deserved. The Mantis liked to order drinks and stare at me as if my paying was a given. She did heap praise on me for my work in children's disabilities and remarked that she just couldn't understand how a guy like me could be unattached and on a dating site. She kissed me first, took me outside, and jerked me off in the parking lot.

After I returned the Mantis to her house, I looked her up online beyond the dating site and saw that she was in a relationship with a man that seemed pretty appropriate for her status in life. Colorful mohawk and everything. I instantly regretted it but on a drunken impulse I emailed him and let him know his girl was messing around. I didn't care, wasn't surprised, and didn't feel invested, so I can't account for why I decided to stir the pot and cook up a whole lot of anger and resentment. I woke up to a barrage of texts from the Mantis telling me what a loser I am, that I need counseling, that I failed at ruining her life, that she and her man are just sitting in his home laughing together over how pathetic I am, and that I'm the reason women are afraid to meet men from the Internet. I didn't respond but also didn't predict the limitless energy the Mantis had to keep harassing me over the next two weeks. Each time I thought about blocking her I also thought she'd just tire herself out, but was proven wrong when after a few days she needed to again let me know that I didn't screw her over and that I'm still a loser.

I didn't feel like a loser until the afternoon of Isabella's birthday when I finally got around to realizing she was a pretty good match for me, and I tried to come back into her focus after fading out of her life. Isabella didn't hesitate to let me know she was no longer interested and would rather spend her birthday alone. She's gone on to win dance competitions, work in embassies, and is still traveling the world. The most attention I've gone on to receive is when I got stuck in an elevator and rescued by the fire department. Isabella left me with a gift and a lot to think about. I had to think about my priorities and core values, and the gift was realizing there is more to life than getting jerked off in a parking lot and being the reason women are afraid to meet men from the Internet.

CHAPTER FIFTEEN

Tenth Lover – Jordan (Credit Union Teller)

I took a year to get something serious going with another woman. I browsed the same profiles again and again and wondered why these lifers on the dating site hadn't encountered success by now. If online dating worked as advertised, plenty of these women should have met somebody. I made an account registered as a woman so I could see what type of men were out there and a huge swath of the population seemed like people with whom women would want to start relationships. I assumed I was a high quality guy until I clicked through handsome dentists, geologists, and engineers. Jordan's actions would come to help me understand what women want from men these days, in times when it takes two people's income to make a nice living and when women can effortlessly outperform men all over society and access everything they want on their own. Jordan was a lifer despite her having concocted a profile that said in no uncertain terms she would only consider serious offers from relationship minded men.

I met Jordan during the blue period of her dating. Her profile wound down with some sad thoughts about where all the good guys went and how all she wants is to be in a long term committed relationship. I messaged her and said I was likewise underwhelmed by the hookup culture online and wishing I could enjoy a reciprocal relationship free of worrying over how soon my partner was going to need the high that only comes from sparking with somebody new. Jordan said my message was thoughtful and suggested we take her little girl to the zoo as friends so she could better explain her home life situation. Jordan was five years younger and turned out to be taller than me despite saying she was shorter online. Her presentation and personality were mousey and submissive but under scrutiny I could tell she misrepresented things online to advance her goals. She was living with her baby daddy but packaged herself as single, saying she and the father both considered themselves broken up but in a holding pattern until they could afford separate housing. Clearly, she was in a relationship but willing to jump ship if she'd land on a faster boat to paradise.

Jordan had obscenely large boobs while maintaining a slender waist and flat stomach. Jordan was basically the image of beauty that throngs of women point to in the media as damaging and not attainable. Well, Jordan attained it. I guess that shape isn't an unrealistic ideal of beauty. Jordan usually wore bejeweled jeans and a tank top with spaghetti straps that strained to contain her delicious melons. I didn't set out to find a woman with Jordan's measurements, and had never pursued anyone over their body type alone, but having the gold standard shinning right in my face blinded me to all that was so obviously wrong with her desire to have it all. Jordan would frequently come to my apartment distressed because of an argument she had to have with her baby daddy just to get out the door. It was evident that the man didn't consider them broken up and was constantly confronting her over her actions. Jordan dismissed my questions and assured me that when she saved enough money she was going to move out. Except she worked part time at a credit union and spent all her money frivolously. I could see why the man would feel anxiety as Jordan slipped away from him, as she was unbelievably attractive and only aspired to play house and provide domestic comfort.

True to her statement that she wanted to be in a long term relationship, Jordan immediately began spending every day at my apartment, and sleeping over each night that the baby daddy was responsible for their daughter. Jordan filled my fridge and pantry with food and shopping, and provided a meal schedule for when we would have pasta, casserole, fajitas and so on. I knew this living was fake but enjoyed it nonetheless. I even invited friends and coworkers over certain nights so Jordan could entertain, and project her image of being a homemaker. In addition to cooking and cleaning for me, Jordan also provided ample quality time with her glorious boobs. She walked around in nighties and almost as if our domestic schedule demanded intimacy she'd call me over and announce it was time for sex, revealing her best assets to put me in the mood. Jordan could effortlessly make a whole dick disappear down her throat and for all her inconsistencies she did not exaggerate her ability to make home life blissful.

Jordan put all this effort into making our very short term relationship feel established and long term. Her irritable qualities were limited to a general disinterest in world affairs, how long she could prattle on about why I needed to leave my bank for a credit union, and how the only movies she enjoyed starred Adam Sandler and Kevin James. Jordan had been a teller forever and was perfectly content standing at her window all day, reading celebrity gossip on her phone when members weren't around. One night while Jordan was serving us dinner, I tried to shake up our routine with a serious conversation about national politics. She expressed utter confusion so I tested her high school education and probed for whether or not she could name a branch of the government. Jordan hesitated for several painful minutes and then asked if judicial-ary was a thing. She then got irked and enforced our schedule of dinner, dishes, the sophomoric humored movie and lovemaking.

Drilling Jordan for more than a surface level perfect partnership eroded her resolve and the following night she decided to point out ways in which I wasn't inputting the masculine energy needed to match her output of feminine energy, which was causing her a lopsided and dysfunctional relationship. She felt like she was making food and being beautiful and although I was complimenting her sufficiently I wasn't making the right financial sacrifices. Jordan explained her expected tiers of gift giving, and said that she wanted special larger gifts for occasions like birthdays, anniversaries and holidays, and sporadic smaller gifts for thinking-of-you moments and incidents of me wanting to remind her that she is cherished and adored. She then doubled down on the lesson and said flowers are tricky as a gift because the wrong variety will offend her, especially anything from her classification of weeds, and to never forget she is a grown woman and therefore has no use for balloons and stuffed animals. She wrapped up by warning that despite what I think I know about Valentine's Day, the only correct present is jewelry. I shed a single tear for womankind and though I was thoroughly entertained I told her I got it. I secretly decided to tread water in this relationship until Jordan realized I wasn't going to buy her anything from her wish list of appeasements and leave me.

It didn't take long after that talk for Jordan to find the door. Especially when I dropped my own bomb on her. I got fed up with my employers at the mental and behavioral health company and walked off the job without having anything else lined up or so much as a cent in savings. Dumbfounded, Jordan kept asking for an explanation and I kept telling her that the company had intensified its dedication to evil and was now piling up kids with conflicting diagnoses in an improperly named summer camp, and asking me to babysit this dangerous melee so I could fraudulently bill for all day long group therapy. I told her that older boys with aggressive sexualized behaviors were showing younger non-verbal children with Autism their penises and that somebody was going to get hurt. And somebody did get hurt but thankfully it was only a female staff. There were strong, irritable and easily triggered older boys that should not have been asked to participate in this disgusting money grab. Besides, I told Jordan, I was a highly skilled clinician now asked to drive a 15 passenger van and come up with ways to torture children all day so the company could pretend to have a therapeutic summer program and rake in the profits. Jordan got angry and told me I was being ridiculous because money is important.

The first thing I did while unemployed was motivate myself by watching films like Braveheart, Gladiator and the Shawshank Redemption. I kept my spirit up by miming lines about how every man dies but not every man really lives, get busy living or get busy dying, and freeeeeeeedom. I hadn't really noticed that Jordan disappeared until she called me up and asked me to meet her at Beyond Bread. I knew what was coming. I met Jordan for dinner and she informed me that we were each going to buy our own meal. I wasn't hungry so I ordered a small side of pasta salad while she ordered a meat chili. Her hands trembled slightly as she smashed crackers into her bowl and the quiver in her voice was just noticeable as she told me she only wanted to be friends from here and that she was no longer romantically attracted to me. I praised her for her courage and told her that nobody had ever afforded me such dignity in a breakup before. I agreed aloud that we could remain friends but knew that sex was the only thing that had kept me interested this long. Jordan had no passions we could mine for conversations and if we weren't fucking then something like common interests would suddenly become important.

I deleted my dating profile recognizing the need to divert that time and energy to jobing and employment websites. Still, there were women out there who had been talking to me and with some I had already exchanged phone numbers or personal email addresses. One determined mulatto young woman with a strong spiritual side pushed to meet me despite me cautioning her I was a career-less bum. She insisted on buying me a meal and had also brought me a Tupperware container full of her original tofu salad. This Oracle told me to relax and said that the universe was telling her everything for me was going to work out. She assured me that I still had a career in children's welfare services and that I was simply between jobs. The Oracle wanted to date me and extended an invitation to sleep at her house right away, saying we could go swimming and then do a reading that might help me on my journey. Ultimately, I declined because I saw another situation where she was always going to be more attracted to me than I was to her but I did appreciate her providing a boost to my self esteem. I only took 30 days to get hired at a religious non-profit for a substantial cut in pay, but the organization and class of people I was going to work with soared above the mental and behavioral health company I flipped off.

Back to that evening at Beyond Bread, Jordan's final confession boggled my mind. She ended our breakup by telling me that the baby daddy discovered her dating profile and responded by pressing her against a brick wall and choking her to where she thought she might pass out. Jordan said that was the romantic gesture she had been looking for from him and determined that he was willing to try harder to be in a relationship. She said they wanted to give love another chance and were going to try and be a family again (which didn't work out, and she soon joined a niche dating service promising to find women their sugar daddies). Jordan just wanted a dick to suck in exchange for praise and presents, and knowing this moved me to shed a second tear. I didn't cry for womankind but wept because this woman's huge boobs had previously enamored me enough to actually pay money for an Adam Sandler and Kevin James ticket and I can never not say I didn't see Grown Ups 2 in the theater.

CHAPTER SIXTEEN

Eleventh Lover – Kyra (Businesswoman)

I met Kyra during a fruitful season of online dating, so probably around the holidays when women seem to initiate more messages. We set a date but then women I was more attracted to began filling up my calendar and I came to think of meeting Kyra as a chore. When the time came, I met Kyra at the restaurant but found myself completely uninterested in her. I felt badly about this and did my best to answer her questions and listen to her stories but felt no chemistry. Before I escaped this date, Kyra hooked me with the revelation that her company had a community giving program that many of the children and families in my social work caseload needed. So, without fully intending to, I gave Kyra false hope and sent enough mixed signals to keep her tuned into helping me help my clients. As long as she thought she was going to get laid, she'd swiftly handle my referrals and my clients would reap the benefits in a New York minute. In the future, she'd break down and holler at me to remember the difference between her personal and professional phone numbers. Kyra's time line with me weaves in between my last two relationships.

Kyra was average looking but I had just come off a stretch of dating beautiful women and she lacked the certain je ne sais quoi to really attack my attention. She had a thicker body and what she described as mermaid hair, which was brown, wavy, and voluminous. Kyra's photos from the dating site played to her strengths and she did a great job dressing up as a woodland fairy for Halloween, but in real life she either dressed like a businesswoman or a gypsy depending on whether she was working or playing. She had just left the Peace Corps and was proud to have secured her first professional job. Perhaps due to her young age, she was quick to brag about her income and the ability to pay bills on time and have enough left over to play with and save. While knowing her, she bought an expensive car and gave it a stupid nickname. It's just a fact of life that the women I date make loads more money than I do. It seems society will pay for many products and services ten times before doling out dollars to the people tending to disenfranchised children. I could boost my income several levels by starting in fast food and sticking around long enough to wear an assistant manager's hat. Until I go that route, I have to derive all my job satisfaction from putting good back into the world. The only perk social workers have going for them is the flexibility to work and live life simultaneously. I spend most my working hours in the community and can manage my own amusement and obligations betwixt whatever I'm doing for the job. Kyra, in addition to being chubby and decorating herself with bling, was also sarcastic. The well intentioned jokes at my expense pushed her rating with me from average to below.

At the height of my working collaboration with Kyra, she came to one of my office buildings and gave a presentation for which I received many accolades. My bosses thanked me for finding her organization as a resource and then fostering the professional relationship. I knew Krya was due a fuck in gratitude and decided that when my then girlfriend left me I'd give her a call. When the time came, I made sure I dialed Kyra's personal line and told her she could come help me get over the woman that just broke my heart. The heartbreak was a slight exaggeration as what had happened was I quit my job at the mental and behavioral health company and the superficial siren I was with said I could no longer afford her. Krya was ready to get sworn in so to speak and showed up with little notice. When I answered the door, I immediately felt the pangs of regret. Kyra tried to look nice in anticipation of sex but all I saw was my buyer's remorse. She arrived with groceries, and offered an impressive supply of unique beers she thought I'd enjoy. Kyra's gifts made me feel like an asshole since I immediately knew I did not want to get physical with her. My mind raced for an exit and turned toward hoping Kyra misunderstood my original message to mean I wanted companionship and a pep talk as a cure for loneliness. Nope. Kyra informed me that she has a latex allergy and so brought us a supply of lambskin condoms. Lovely.

Self preservation took over, and I brought out a series of animated superhero movies that would take us awhile to finish and hopefully outlast Krya's hormones. Impressively, she watched two full DVD's with me before making her move. After a logical enough time to become tired, I started yawning and slumping over as if I were struggling to stay awake. Unfortunately, Kyra saw my drifting off as a clarion call to action and made her now or never pass at me. She started kissing my neck (disgusting) and rubbing my dick (kinda not bad). Kyra aroused me enough that I would gladly accept a blow job but of course she put one of those hippie condoms on me and connected us via our primary sex organs. She wasn't comfortable with me seeing her naked and had left panties out of the ensemble for unobstructed access. The lack of confidence piled on top of the sarcasm turned me off even more and I went soft inside of her. I said aloud that I was tired but she could try and revive me if she were up to it. Kyra finally put her mouth on my penis and started sucking, which was a nice reprieve from listening to her sarcastic comments about my apartment. She was pretty good at fellatio, undoubtedly from guys not wanting to have sex with her, and I came quickly. When the blood flowed back into my brain, I felt incredible guilt because I knew there was no way I was prepared to pay this bill with any part of my body. And yet we bargained.

Would I go down on her? No. Too tired and may get dizzy. Would I finger her? No. Too much keyboard and now Carpal tunnel syndrome. Would I get hard again? Not likely since I skipped a meal earlier. I pushed her down gently and rubbed her back for awhile, pretending out loud that I was giving her a sensual massage. I feigned a few more yawns and Krya finally got the hint that she needed to leave. I apologized and blamed my poor performance on being an early thirties male, saying I missed the bounce back time of my twenties, passing on to her the hollow advice to never get old. I walked Kyra to her dumb car that looked like an egg on wheels and even after all that awkwardness she still gave me a sloppy goodnight kiss. As she drove off, I deleted both her numbers. The children I serve at work were just going to have to be happy having me and whatever supportive services I could find and muster for them that didn't involve whoring myself out to whooties.

CHAPTER SEVENTEEN

Twelfth Lover – Liberty (Home Aide)

The few times I've been curious enough to register a dating profile as a female have left me feeling sick to my stomach. I've only ever wanted to see the men with whom I'm competing, and there are some decent profiles out there, but within seconds of online activity a shit bomb detonates in my fake mailbox and I have at least ten messages asking if I want immediate contact with a penis. Maybe worse than that are the 50 messages that follow which are more respectful in tone but still so obviously crafted to achieve the same result. Online dating mirrors nature in that men pursue and women choose but the semi-anonymity a screen name provides also gives certain men the disgusting confidence needed to lob proposals at women who would be better off not standing in the line of fire. Just like casinos and the lottery, I have to reason that maybe there are enough success stories out there to keep women coming back thinking they will somehow sift through the chaff, beat the odds, and find true love. The next two women that became my sexual partners were both fresh from abusive dating nightmares, leaving me simultaneously flattered that I seemed trustworthy enough to risk getting back on the saddle after a major trauma but also wondering why finding a man is so important when a woman's life otherwise seems to be going well.

Liberty makes the only date I've ever gone on from the second most popular online dating site. I basically copied my same profile from the polished and more popular site and dumped everything into that messy site with its terrible user interface and even worse mobile app. Liberty wrote to me right away and shared that she wasn't very savvy with online dating but was hoping to meet a nice boyfriend. Her pictures looked cute, showed her to spend a lot of time outside, and even previewed her body in the occasional yoga pose. Her hair was very short which looked good on her and she always seemed to be smiling and having a good time without being photographed in a bar surrounded by floozies and alcohol. A couple photos were from a marathon she ran where she and a bestie decorated themselves in tutus and brightly splattered paints. Liberty was cool enough to meet and her naivety gave me the impression she hadn't yet been spoiled by an abundant amount of off putting men. In reality, her couple of bad experiences before me qualified as the worst of the worst.

Liberty worked a human services job not unlike something I had previously acquired for my clients with developmental disabilities. She essentially had a few families assigned to her of which she would cook, clean and tend to the disabled members for a few hours on various weekdays. She also went to school to advance her standing in the field. We met at a coffee shop one night after her class let out and she breathed a sigh of relief when she saw me. She sat next to me and scooted up close and was immediately at ease. Liberty warned that she considered herself awkward and apologized for wearing black yoga pants and a pink tank top, saying she had a scrubby and rushed day. I can't say that I've ever been disappointed by yoga pants on a nice ass and told her to relax. Asking an online date about past online dates is a quick conversation starter but it also spotlights that the date at hand isn't a natural interaction and for me doesn't build a lasting rapport. Still, in Liberty's case, I wondered aloud why she was supposedly having a difficult time of things and got to hear her two incredible stories. Oh, and the only statement she made that backed up her claim of being awkward was when out of nerves she tacked onto her introduction a warning that she very easily gets pregnant.

Liberty said that in the beginning of her online dating, she felt like she had to give everyone who wrote to her a chance. The first gentleman suitor offered to take her to an Italian restaurant, so she prepped herself nicely and went out hoping for a romantic dinner. She said the man ordered several appetizers, ate quickly, and then excused himself to the restroom for an inordinate amount of time. The wait staff then informed Liberty that her date wasn't returning, had previously pulled the same stunt on other women, and if she chose not to pay for the food then the table's waitress would have to foot the bill. Liberty said she asked for the leftovers to be boxed up and settled the check. I felt badly for her and liked the idea that she took the effort to choose me rather than just meeting me because I tossed her a message. Then she told me the really frightening story.

The second gentleman suitor that courted Liberty out from behind her computer monitor was a peevish little man she wasn't particularly attracted to that really made her life a living hell. This guy apparently formed a strong covalent bond to Liberty after just one date and immediately started blowing up her phone and appearing at her work. She felt uncomfortable enough that her employer took steps to increase her personal safety and made other workers aware of the unfolding situation and established rules for response if an incident occurred. The persistent pervert began registering social media profiles in Liberty's name and likeness and went about adding all her friends and relatives only to bombard them with lewd comments and spam. I later searched Liberty's name and sure enough I saw her cloned profiles all over the place all broadcasting her home address and phone number and encouraging strangers to rape and murder her. Sitting with Liberty in the coffee shop, I had to ask how much time had passed since she resolved all this and was startled to learn the threat was very much alive and active. Liberty shrugged off that her stalker could very well be in the parking lot. I tried to hide how pissed off I was to have been dragged into her drama unwittingly and asked why she so comfortably added my life to this heap of danger. Liberty scoffed at my concern and assured me that I could definitely take the little fucker if he attacked me. Excuse me, what if he confronted me with a samurai sword or battery acid or some shit?

For some reason (pussy), I saw Liberty one more time but did take steps to ensure more safety. We met at a park in the middle of a weekend and she cooked us a very delicious pasta picnic. She possibly could have been a successful long term match for me if dating her didn't mean I'd inherit a scary stalker and invite torture and misery into mine and my family's lives. In just the few days between dates, Liberty had appeared in court for a restraining order but was not granted one after the stalker failed to show. No, he instead waited outside for her and threw some ambitious punches before her screams stirred the police to come and make an arrest. Knowing that my potential murder was at least a few days out due to my date's enraged chaser sitting in a jail cell helped recharge my libido. I made out with Liberty and she lamented that previous dates hadn't been on par with my charm and sex appeal. She said she was relieved to know I thought she was attractive and offered to follow me back to my place for an afternoon fuck. I asked if she were sure, given that she still didn't know me too well and had nothing but bad luck in the past, and she retorted in jest that if I didn't strike while she was hot then she may think better of it and rescind. I told her I didn't live too far.

In my apartment, Liberty commented that it felt good standing in a bachelor pad. I don't really think of my place as such but good for her. She then disclosed that she didn't want me to freak out but that I needed to know she was a recent breast cancer survivor, her short hair having grown back from being fully bald, and that she also has mild leukemia. I didn't freak out, and had by now deduced as much from her pink ribbon tattoo, and just thought shit goddamn this girl is a massive train wreck. Liberty then unrolled her expectation that if I was going to fuck her then I needed to fuck her super hard like I was unconcerned about breaking her fragile body. I told her I thought I could manage and then lived up to my word. Her cancer free boobs looked and felt normal and I was happy to finally meet her butt apart from the yoga pants. If Liberty's stalker was going to murder me then it wasn't going to happen before I murdered Liberty's vagina. While she was screaming in pleasure and moaning in ecstasy she demanded to know where this aggressive half of my personality had been hiding all afternoon, delighting in what a wonderful surprise it was to get absolutely slammed. Could this simple act be why women put themselves in perpetual danger? In the penultimate moments of an exhausting bang, she took the condom off and directed my exploding cum into her eager mouth.

I enjoyed the sex, too, and after Liberty left weighed the pros and cons of seeing her again. On the pro side, she was a good cook and better lover. On the con side, were the future maimed corpses of everyone I cared about. Fortunately for me, Liberty took herself out of contention and, much later, shockingly informed me that her stalker raped her and got her pregnant leaving her too embarrassed to pursue me. The only follow up I made after that was a quick visit to her profile where I viewed some ultrasound photos and read corresponding captions she wrote with her familiar optimism. The old fake profiles were still littered around but the search results didn't appear as if new iterations were being created. Hopefully the absence of ongoing fraudulent activity meant the rapist finally faced a real consequence. The situation, in Liberty's telling, certainly painted law enforcement in a negative light. I know from social work that the restraining order process frequently causes the stalked to feel like they're being asked to stalk the stalkers. Liberty's original task was to find her tormentor and serve him with the pre-restraining order, with the caveat that she could call an officer for help only if she had the subject in her sight. For Liberty to have been beaten up outside of court and then raped at her house all after she had originally filed a complaint leaves a lot of questions unanswered. Or maybe her whole story was bullshit. I mean, she'd have to be a little crazy to fuck that good.

CHAPTER EIGHTEEN

Thirteenth Lover – Mallory (Tango Instructor)

I didn't date much while starting my new job at the religious non-profit. Although the job itself was in no way difficult, I primarily focused on quickly building up a body of quality work so I could enjoy the trust and freedom that comes with competence and results. Reestablishing a work reputation went well and life overall was infinitely better than it was with the mental and behavioral health company. And even though my new office was 95 percent female, I vowed to never pursue another coworker and try really hard not to be my hallway's creepy guy. Still, despite higher job satisfaction and the free time to become reacquainted with hobbies and friends, loneliness reared its ugly head and caused me to resurrect my profile.

Ironically, the next woman to ask me out worked for a company very similar to the one I had just left. Before I met her I guessed Mallory was going to be strung out from job stress, and the idea that she would have limited time away from her case management duties appealed to me because I wanted to mostly carry on with my new job and old friends. Trying to set a date with Mallory was easy for me due to the aforementioned freedom but revealed she had even fewer open nights because, on top of a demanding job, she also spent several evenings teaching tango dance classes. Mallory was a few years older than me but she wrote lively messages and displayed pictures showing off Argentine tango moves that tickled my imagination.

Mallory came into the coffee shop the night of our first date looking very nice in black work clothes and a stylish short haircut. She brought overflowing enthusiasm which really made the date enjoyable. I liked that the conversation flowed, she genuinely made me laugh, and I could relate to her job without any longer holding the same responsibilities. Mallory giggled, initiated touches, and kept handing me her phone to take pictures of her for social media. I had a good enough time to see her again, and knew she wouldn't be bothering me too much in the time between dates. Mallory came to the movie theater the night of our second date again looking very nice, as she knew how to elevate her appearance with the right wardrobe. She brought back the enthusiasm but also a weird surprise. When we found our seats she exclaimed for me to check something out and then discharged a taser so close to my leg that the electrical current felt hot. Mallory said she would explain later why she needed to arm herself with weapons before dates.

By the time the movie ended and I kissed Mallory, I had already forgotten about her self defense initiative. I think it is entirely reasonable for women to consider their safety on dates with strangers, especially after the fiasco that was my last date whereby secondhand stalking fears made my own life uncomfortable. But Mallory wanted to tell me a story so we sat in her car and I listened to yet another woman's shocking rape testimony. Mallory said she met a man from our dating website and liked him enough to visit his apartment. She said he served her a drink which made her feel immediately tired, like heavy sleep was rolling over her. Her memories include being led into his bedroom, assumptions that she was innocently assisted into bed for sleep, but then being flipped onto her stomach and having sex despite trying to say no. Mallory said the morning after was full of confusion and vomiting, and that the man had forcefully woken her up and returned her to her vehicle while she still struggled to walk. She said she went back to see him the next night, thinking she needed to apologize if she had gotten sick while at his place, but then figured out she was most likely drugged and asked him about it. His response was to break her phone and punch her in the head. Mallory had to run outside screaming, where the attention from neighbors probably saved her life. She went to the police and was provided a rape kit but never pressed any charges. I didn't know what Mallory could possibly want from me at this point, just a few weeks removed from her assault, but before I could excuse myself out of her car she grabbed me to resume making out.

I read a lot of blogs at work, and many of them are run by the dominant feminist community, and am familiar with what is the politically correct way to talk about the hookup culture but, make no mistake, here I met two consecutive women who made light of their safety and baited their hooks with the thought that I should be pleased they wanted to be with me so soon after a dangerous affair. With Mallory, I would have preferred to go slowly and assess whether we could see ourselves together in the future before she cast me as her next lover following such a nightmare but she suggested getting together at my place and made it clear she was all in. She also started schooling me unprovoked in grammar and other topics which got under my skin and left me feeling like she could take things as far as she wanted and then deal with the consequences if and when I decided to pull a fade on her. Mallory paid lip service to her ordeal and, despite no pressure from me, cautioned that it would take her some time before she could trust another person enough to be intimate with them. Mallory's referendum amounted to 30 minutes of small talk on my couch before she issued an executive order telling me to remove her pants. I think she wanted me to see her G-string because she told me she only wears those and that her style of dance necessitates certain panties.

Sex with Mallory was surprisingly great! Her vagina was extremely condom friendly, and when I praised how tight she was she sighed and said other guys had raved about her privates and she guessed she was simply built small down there. Unfortunately, Mallory's eagerness to correct my speech and challenge my foundation of knowledge got old fast and easily overtook my interest in sex from her. We only did it twice, and by the second time I cared so little that in the same day before I saw her I also donated the maximum amount of plasma. I approached the sex earnestly but immediately realized my extremities were listless and numb and the gold member service was off the menu. I confessed that plasmapheresis sapped me of my strength, and Mallory accommodated by climbing on top. All I had to do was lie there and, again, receive superior pleasure from her tighter than average vagina. Double unfortunately, Mallory reminded me today was her birthday but now asked if I would consider joining her at a dinner with friends and coworkers. She came over having omitted that a celebration was scheduled and possibly planned all along to guilt me into participating. I picked myself up off the bed, now drained from having donated fluids twice, put on the same clothes, and lackadaisically sprayed myself down with aerosol freshener.

Mallory's birthday party was at Blanco's Tacos in La Encantada, which is a trendy spot to eat and socialize for most college graduates and young professionals but squarely inside my places to never go to database as I always try and avoid the restaurants and bars overcrowded with my fellow young people. I also found it ironic that I quit my job to get away from mental and behavioral healthcare providers and now I was attending a case manager's birthday party made up of all her female coworkers. The party from start to finish was nothing but screaming chicks and all I could do was pick at chips and salsa while scanning the room for the occasional sympathetic glace from a table busser. Eventually, Mallory's cabal made its way to the parking lot where I had to stand around for longer as the drunk and giddy women took turns playing with Mallory's damn taser. Finally, Mallory drove me home and thanked me for contributing to such a fulfilling evening for her. She told me she craved security in a relationship and that the night for her foreshadowed good things. I realized that I, too, wanted somebody to spend birthdays with and come home to but that this person would never be Mallory, whose attractiveness to me was in free fall. I remained sensitive to Mallory's feelings and with acknowledgment to her taser decided that I would delve deeply into my thoughts and dig up the most dignified way out of this relationship for both of us.

The next time Mallory texted me to hangout I told her I had an unforgiving bout of diarrhea.

CHAPTER NINETEEN

Fifteenth Lover – Ophelia (Cultural Studies Professor)

A buxom redhead from the online dating site had been making plans with me for a first date when an honest-to-god missed message broke up our conversation. Unlike the times I pretended not to get somebody's mail, I just didn't see that she sent me a thoughtful email proposing some dinner spots and was pleasantly surprised when she got in touch with me again a couple weeks later to draw back my attention. By now, another woman and I were in the burgeoning stage of a dating relationship and had plans for the same afternoon the redhead wanted to meet but we weren't serious enough yet that adding on a second date would feel wrong. Or I felt badly enough about the missed message that a sense of obligation clouded my judgment. I technically would have met Ophelia first, so to make up for the technical difficulties I scheduled a dating doubleheader.

My first date tired me out and then I met Ophelia and felt guilty upon realizing she brought her A-game. Ophelia selected a gourmet hamburger restaurant from feedback I provided on my tastes and she showed up ready to carry a date. A lot of first dates scheduled online feel like pre-dates where two people haphazardly meet for coffee to talk nonsense and assess the possibility of a more involved real date in the future but Ophelia wore a long strapless dress, wrestled her foxy red hair into place, and put forward her best face. She greeted me with enthusiasm, talked to the servers like she was out for a romantic evening, and made plenty of admissions that she was finding herself attracted to me. I liked her, too, despite just having come from seeing a woman with whom I shared indelible chemistry. However, the woman from my afternoon lived two hours away and I didn't know how practical pursuing a relationship with her would be and so felt a degree of relief in meeting a well-rounded redhead a little closer to home.

Our first date concluded with a quiet walk around downtown and a simple goodnight kiss. The evening stayed light, fun, and was never awkward. Fortunately or unfortunately, sparks with the other woman exploded and laid waste to Ophelia's efforts to stay in touch with me. About two months went by before I was single again but also heartbroken from the shattered relationship lying in the immediate past. More than anything, I reached out to Ophelia hoping for a distraction and found she was willing to come out on another date after so much time gone by. This new first date with Ophelia was awkward because I had to make up an excuse to cover having fallen off the map and misleadingly warn her I had given up all my vices as part of a new healthy living strategy when in reality I felt so down I was willing to try anything and had read online that going 90 days without caffeine, alcohol and masturbation could cure anybody of what ails them. After some devastating withdrawals, the benefits of natural homeostasis set in and I did start to feel healthier and re-energized without artificial happiness coursing through my body, and I was able to strike a pleasant groove with Ophelia, too. We went on some winsome dates and she still skewed toward doing things that made me happy, like seeing Guardians of the Galaxy, despite her own interests being more academic and hoity-toity.

Then Ophelia capriciously revealed herself to be a huge liberal douchebag. Apparently I had been dating her in the dwindling days of her summer vacation, and when graduate school restarted she began telling horror stories about the University of Arizona taking too long to activate her keycard, attitude given to her by the tech support guys after she scolded them for not setting up a website to her liking, and generally how she sees herself as the most important and hardest working steward of humanity waking up each morning. Ophelia's studies and degrees all had to do with women's issues in the African and Native American communities and she tried to get me to understand how important she was to her vaguely filled out notion of progress. Since I do social work in the areas Ophelia thinks she leaves an impact, I could quietly laugh to myself knowing nobody asked Ophelia to take up a cause for them. As if there's a black or Tohono O'odham family out there grateful for this isolated white lady's sacrifice of time typing up shit over the weekend on her MacBook Air. Riiight.

I've voted for more democrats than republicans but what makes Ophelia the Queen of Liberal Douchebags is the stream of inconsistency in her worldview and the actions she takes to project enlightenment that then blow up in her face. My absolute favorite of Ophelia's sob stories is her retelling of how her mother-in-law helped kill her ten month marriage to the King of Liberal Douchebags. Ophelia apparently married a similarly motivated idiot whose academic ambitions started paying off before hers and when he had to choose between slowing down and supporting his wife's goals or taking off and getting douchier accolades on his own he chose to cast Ophelia aside and take his douchey solo act to the big time. The mother-in-law had all along voiced opposition to Ophelia and King's gender neutral relationship but never more so than the day of the wedding ceremony. When the minister announced the couple's married title and revealed that the lovebirds legally hyphenated both of their last names together, Ophelia's new mother-in-law turned heads and ruined the video recording by yelling out: WHAT THE FUCK IS THAT SHIT?

Despite realizing everything I told my friends and coworkers about Ophelia was to get a laugh at her expense, I just couldn't do away with a warm body while still hurting and longing for my recently lost true love interest. On around the 30th day of my abstinence challenge, Ophelia told me my intentions were bullshit and asserted that I was senselessly depriving her of intimacy. She said she'd still date me without sex but made it clear she'd be happier if we fucked. She also shared her belief that if sucking dick were an Olympic event then she'd make our country proud. I took Ophelia's feelings into consideration and invited her over for a movie and one of those bragged about gold medal blow jobs, and after confirming her claim that she swallows a cock like a champion I did my best to take some pleasure back to her court. Try as I might, I couldn't get over how my last lover was a decade younger than me, milky smooth, happy, bubbly, and refreshing to be with while Ophelia was my same age down to my exact date of birth, grumpy, spoiled, obnoxious, a shameless self promoter, and now slightly chubs from a perpetual college diet of fast food after midnight. It only took two nights of gross sex with Ophelia before I decided I'd rather be alone than with somebody whose improved plan for her next gender neutral marriage is to sit with her husband and randomly generate a new last name.

Bless my lucky star, Ophelia went away on her own. A challenger to the throne of douchedom appeared from within her cultural studies circle and swept her off her feet. I'm sure they'll be happy together, disappoint each other's parents plenty, publish a volume of boring papers, and possibly offend a lot of minorities.

CHAPTER TWENTY

Fourteenth Lover – Nevaeh (Store Manager)

Be careful with online dating. For awhile, I felt like the sorcerer's apprentice from Fantasia trying to put away the magic. It can't be done and people get hurt.

If the goal of online dating is to find the love of your life and enter into a relationship with them then I succeeded. Twice. The same woman, two times. Except it turns out I don't believe in happy endings, and I'd rather just encounter my soulmate once, be able to think of her when I need to, and move forward alone on my path to peaceful oblivion. I met a girl so great that I want to remember her in a bubble and never find ourselves sitting around a table together solving bills, and no longer be of consequence to her when I'm old and shitting myself. There's probably a less perfect person for me and if there isn't then I'm still OK. Every human is made of seven billion atoms and with mass mostly comprised of oxygen, carbon and hydrogen, and yet somehow the last woman I dated came together in more harmonious construction than anyone else and achieved this perfection without even needing a full five feet of height.

I live in Tucson and Nevaeh lives in Phoenix so we are separated by two hours of driving. I found her on the dating site after I depleted my supply of local women and the algorithm started recommending matches from outlying areas. The whole endeavor seemed comical by now and after finally gaining a degree of shame I was nearly ready to delete my account for good. But I messaged Nevaeh because she was just so freaking cute, with her short stature and oversized smile, and she wrote back quickly. We fell into a fast back and forth conversation and before long she provided her phone number and began texting me. She alerted me to her upcoming birthday and I reflexively added that information into her profile on my phone. Which is also the only reason we stayed in contact, because after a lull in our communication and never making plans to break down the distance my phone reminded me to wish her happy birthday. I now know, from the benefit of dating her, that the birthday greeting was a well received pivotal moment following a series of missteps she had been taking in her dating life. Nevaeh and I agreed to meet, and she volunteered for the first car trip.

Nevaeh is a decade younger than me. She is 22 and I am 32. She also has a three year old son whose dad is, you guessed it, an asshole from the Border Patrol. Nevaeh, having come from a tumultuous multicultural upbringing and then finding herself a teen mom, was still able to do very well for herself. She stuck with her high school job in a girls' clothing store long enough to become its general manager, making far more money than I ever could doing social work. The discrepancy in pay and already knowing of her chain from its controversy in selling sexualized styles to prepubescent girls, not unlike the ones on my caseload, was initially unsettling. But Nevaeh couldn't be nicer and from her perspective she makes the little girls who come into her store feel good about themselves. And since she picked me to date out of all her options her success fed my male ego. Unfortunately for spending time together her job stole all of her attention and so our first date actually played out in slivers over a week, culminating with her sleeping over before we even had a full conversation. She simply walked in my apartment door and spoiled me with the sugariest lips I ever met.

I did temporarily lose control of Nevaeh's sex drive. She is absolutely insatiable and although I could keep up with her the first night, my confidence began to wither in each subsequent encounter and I acquired fear that I'd perform even worse the next. We shared such passion and chemistry that we devoured each other every chance we got but she kept going way past my empty tank. I was also driving myself crazy trying to see her multiple times a week, tacking on sleepovers to work trips that only took me halfway to her. While the relationship was still new and full of limerence, I did something unbelievably stupid and sent her a letter saying long distance dating wouldn't work. When she confronted me with my cowardice, we met in Casa Grande, the midpoint between Tucson and Phoenix, to talk. I laid my feelings out that the sex was overwhelming to me and I'd like to get to know each other better, and she seemed to be on board though she texted me later and said I had put too many doubts in her head to move forward as a romantic couple. I was still embarrassed about not being able to get hard for her the last time we had sex, and compensated by sending her one, two or 20 too many pictures of my dick during its recovery. Our text conversations dwindled, I mailed her a couple cards just to let her know I was still thinking about her, but we mostly stopped talking for 50 days.

In the beginning of those 50 days, I annoyed my coworkers with my depression and didn't do much more than feel sorry for myself. My officemate introduced me to Maca Root Extract and told me to take it every day to fan a roaring libido. I implemented this daily supplement, started exercising, did away with alcohol, caffeine and masturbation, and rebuilt myself better than before. When Nevaeh finally said hi, I felt good enough to put this wheezing relationship to death and bluntly told her that I moved onto fucking a redhead. My admission shocked and surprised her but remarkably also won me an invitation to her son's cowboy themed birthday party. Then Nevaeh disappeared again in the days leading up to the party, which left me and my coworkers debating whether I should still go. Common sense said no but the agitator in all of us thought it would be funny to go out in a blaze of glory by showing up as Toy Story's Woody just to make everyone uncomfortable. Except Nevaeh broke her silence a day before the party to make sure I was still coming and I went and left a positive impression on her family members. I was back on Nevaeh's romantic radar as was imminent makeup sex.

Sex with Nevaeh was now euphoric and even better than all previous times. In our first night reunited, I outlasted her and she took a turn waving the white flag of defeat. It was a triumph of the Maca and just how much raw desire I have for this woman. Just the smallest amount of attention from her keeps me happy for days. Her sweet face is burned into my memory when I close my eyes, and I stand in awe of the good humored and accomplished woman she is every day. She has acting aspirations and if she finds the time then I think she will succeed in Hollywood, too. A night with accidental butt sex earned me my first I love you from her and I'll never forget hearing those soft spoken words in her little angelic voice waft out into the night as she fell asleep beside me. Such love is also fertile ground for cognitive dissonance, or the psychological tendency to deny discrepancies between preexisting beliefs and new information.

Time loop stories are so compelling to me because they show how such tiny and seemingly insignificant events can bring about amazing changes to individual or shared histories. So many things had to go right and wrong for Nevaeh and I to get together and back together: A birthday text, a slutty redhead, even a small fire in her store all impacted us coming together from over 100 miles apart. This second time around I didn't go crazy trying to see her as much, which allowed for more planned and reasonable quality time, and I didn't exert myself trying to pleasure her beyond my abilities and she still reported high physical satisfaction. But like H. G. Wells' time traveler, I started noticing cracks in our utopia. For one, Nevaeh chooses to invest in her store at the expense of her home. Her house is condemnable but I didn't notice until after the twentieth or fiftieth time we had sex. I looked around and thought I should be stripped of my child welfare credentials for not seeing the roaches in the pile of dishes cemented to the sink, last year's now roasted Christmas tree sheltering rodents in the backyard, wads of hair from her two fuzzy cats clinging to everything and coming out of my lungs when I coughed, the omnipotent smell of feline waste, the pee stained walls and floor of the two non-functioning bathrooms, the lone hanging shade still affixed to the not originally opaque sliding glass door, the hodgepodge of discarded food in the fridge now giving birth to new genesis, and the rolling hills of trash including the massive garbage mountain I tripped over in the middle of one night. Giving this hardworking single mom the benefit of the doubt, I on three occasions cleaned everything for her and then watched as she recreated the same messes. I couldn't reconcile how she could run a successful business but not pick up for her kid... and the neglect bothered me.

Nevaeh's lifestyle finally impacted my health and well being. When the little boy caught Hand, Foot and Mouth Disease from his cousins, I still went to visit Nevaeh and help take care of him. And even though adults aren't suppose to easily catch Hand, Foot and Mouth Disease, guess which loser immediately broke out in hot red splotches and a nuclear fever? This one. Realizing our renewed relationship remained a deadend and then telling Nevaeh brewed over into a shitstorm. The thing is, Nevaeh makes a great dream girl for me. She is smart, funny, young and beautiful. Nevaeh does not make a great real girl for me. I can't relate to her youthful independence since I was such a late bloomer and neither of us can just pack up and move. Nevaeh took me to the end of my dating journey, showed me the edge of a wonderful universe, but after seven happy months I knew I had to leave. For both of us. On the way out, I suggested some social services she may not be aware of that could help with her son and she rightfully took great offense. I once wondered what it would be like to gaze upon Nevaeh's face as she became my wife, then I made the choice that took her from loving me to detesting me, and in the future she won't even think about me. I don't care how much sense the breakup makes, or how much of my girlfriend's wardrobe reeked of cat urine, seeing our affectionate photos she once boastfully shared with friends on social media come down hurt.

Now it will be a long time if ever before I open another online dating profile.

jasonkinkade1982@gmail.com

http://kinkadejason.tumblr.com/

Please leave a star rating and review.

http://tinyurl.com/LDCDBUM

The End.